The Shoah on screen –

Representing crimes against humanity

Volume 1

Anne-Marie BARON

Council of Europe Publishing

French version:

La Shoah à l'écran – Crime contre l'humanité et représentation

ISBN-10: 92-871-5492-9
ISBN-13: 978-92-871-5492-7

Design: Graphic Design Workshop, Council of Europe
Council of Europe Publishing
F-67075 Strasbourg Cedex

ISBN-10: 92-871-5960-2
ISBN-13: 978-92-871-5960-1
© Council of Europe, June 2006
Printed at the Council of Europe

Contents

Introduction

Over the past twenty years or so, there have been an increasing number of films about the Shoah, reaching more and more viewers. It is as if, fifty years later, a tacit partial ban on cinematic representation of the only systematic, largest numerically, and most heinous genocide in the entire history of humanity has been lifted. This gap has allowed the Shoah to assume its true historical magnitude and the cinema its true place among the arts. The Shoah marked a return to barbarity at a time when civilisation was making progress. Although the problem of evil is much older, the Shoah has removed it from the metaphysical sphere and turned it into a contemporary, real-life collective experience. It also stimulates thought on other crimes against humanity, committed before and since against other human groups. These notions require precise definitions prior to any discussion of representation as such.

1. Genocide and crimes against humanity

In 1948 genocide was officially defined[1] as the crime of destroying or attempting to destroy a national, ethnic, racial or religious group. It is held to be a war crime and a crime against humanity, to which statutory limitations do not apply.[2] The definition drafted by Professor Raphael Lemkin is both broader and more precise: "a coordinated plan of different actions aiming at the destruction of essential foundations of the life of national groups, with the aim of annihilating the groups themselves".[3] There is a difference between genocide, whose aim – declared or not – is to annihilate an ethnic group as such, by whatever means, and a war crime, whose purpose is to destroy enemies during a civil or foreign war. Two basic features of genocide immediately become apparent: it is intentional and it is systematic. However, historians draw a distinction between "intentionalist"

---

1. First by the London Agreement of 8 August 1945 establishing the charter of the Nuremberg International Military Tribunal and then by the United Nations on 9 December 1948. The text reads as follows: "[...] genocide means any of the following acts committed with intent to destroy, in whole or in part, a national, ethnical, racial or religious group, as such:
    (a) Killing members of the group;
    (b) Causing serious bodily or mental harm to members of the group;
    (c) Deliberately inflicting on the group conditions of life calculated to bring about its physical destruction in whole or in part;
    (d) Imposing measures intended to prevent births within the group;
    (e) Forcibly transferring children of the group to another group."
2. Since 26 November 1968, by a new convention which entered into force on 11 November 1970.
3. *Axis Rule in Occupied Europe: Laws of Occupation – Analysis of Government – Proposals for Redress*, Washington, DC, Carnegie Endowment for International Peace, 1944.

genocide, directly intended and exacted upon the victims by the perpetrators, and "bureaucratic" genocide, involving various administrative intermediaries. Moreover, they do not agree on the definition of "uniqueness" concerning the Jewish genocide.

To be even more rigorous, we might draw a distinction between "genocide" and "ethnocide", since the term "genocide" is too closely associated with systematic slaughter and does not cover certain conflicts or acts of repression which have the – sometimes unintended – consequence of wiping out an ethnic group and its culture. Thus war crimes and crimes of conquest should be distinguished from the expulsion or forcible assimilation of a group and the destruction of a cultural or religious identity, which may occur without any actual intent to murder. But however that may be, these are still crimes against humanity as defined in 1945 by the Nuremberg Tribunal,[4] and international justice is beginning to agree on the need to punish and prevent them.

During these so-called modern times, so fertile in collective crimes of all kinds, the cinema, which had previously been regarded as pure entertainment, succeeded in elevating itself from the role of amusement to the status of seventh art. Aesthetic preoccupations transcended technical considerations, and what was originally a fairground entertainment acquired the dignity that it had deserved from the outset. It is thus as both a popular and artistic form that it has assumed the narrative potential of handing down history and applied itself to representing genocide and crimes against humanity. How has it discharged this task? The way in which we study the material should enable us to approach the field of cinematic representation dispassionately. This field clearly raises problems of all kinds: theoretical, moral and aesthetic. And the raising of such problems entails an examination of the nature of cinema.

---

4. In 1945 the Nuremberg Tribunal responsible for trying Nazi leaders defined a crime against humanity as follows: "murder, extermination, enslavement, deportation, and other inhumane acts committed against any civilian population, before or during the war; or persecutions on political, racial or religious grounds in execution of or in connection with any crime within the jurisdiction of the Tribunal, whether or not in violation of the domestic law of the country where perpetrated". The Tribunal specified that it had the power "to try and punish persons who, acting in the interests of the European Axis countries, whether as individuals or as members of organizations, committed", amongst other things, "crimes against humanity". Pierre Truche has provided a modern definition of this concept in the journal *Esprit*: "A crime against humanity is the application of a doctrine denying a group of people their rights as human beings. It is not a crime one person commits against another person but the execution of a concerted plan to exclude some people from the human community. [...] We can single out what sets a crime against humanity apart from other crimes: it is committed systematically pursuant to an ideology which forcibly denies a group of people the right to live out their difference, whether original or acquired, attacking by that very fact the dignity of each of its members and something that is quintessential to the human race. Inhumane treatment, as in any crime, means that the victims' human nature is also challenged and they are rejected by the human community. [...] One single provision makes it [the crime against humanity] subject to special [legal] treatment: it does not come under the statute of limitations, which means that its perpetrators can be prosecuted right up to the day of their death." "La Notion de crime contre l'humanité", *Esprit*, No. 181, 1992.

2. The problem of terminology

Let us first consider how the name "the Shoah" became established for talking about the genocide perpetrated by the Nazis during the Second World War. Television has had a definite media impact in making the public aware of this unprecedented event. A 1978 American television mini-series[5] established the term "holocaust", a word of Greek origin, used in antiquity for animal sacrifices and meaning "wholly burnt", that is, both burnt whole and totally consumed by fire. The holocaust is the fullest of the sacrifices described in Leviticus.[6] The term "holocaust" attaches a religious connotation to the Nazi genocide, turning it into a total collective sacrifice as if the victims were animals sacrificed wholesale to please some obscure god.

The word "Shoah" became established in the wake of Claude Lanzmann's 1985 film. This was perhaps one of the film's most important functions: providing an imperishable name – as it appears in the Book of Isaiah cited in the film's epigraph[7] – for the unnameable. It is an unusual and difficult word,[8] chosen by Lanzmann specifically because, he claims, he did not understand its meaning. It is a non-religious word meaning "overwhelming catastrophe", "utter destruction" or "devastation". Lanzmann thus stripped this genocide of its religious connotation and gave it a name that was short, easy to remember and whose meaning had become established.[9] In this respect, the film is an inaugural act of historic importance. It has deliberately chosen to give a thorough and exclusive description of the "how", the way in which the destruction of the Jews was carried out, thus putting aside any considerations that might detract from the immemorial dimension of the Shoah. By allowing historians and eyewitnesses to speak it has avoided portraying the victims in any way, preferring their immediate testimony, and has made official a word denoting an inexorable process whose stages, defined by Raul Hilberg in his book *The Destruction of the European Jews*,[10] were the same throughout Europe: definition, concentration, expropriation, deportation and extermination of the Jews.

---

5. *Holocaust* by Marvin Chomsky, 1978.
6. Leviticus describes four types of sacrifices (*korbanim*) required of the believer: *olah*, the holocaust, in which the victim is totally consumed by fire and releases an odour destined to ascend towards the deity; *shelamim*, thanksgiving; *hattat*, the sin offering; and *asham*, the guilt offering. The root *olah* means "to rise", "to go up" or "to ascend", and the word refers to what is put on the altar, and therefore carried upwards, since the altar is always on a high place, while the Greek word *holos* means "whole". The word "holocaust" may have been adopted by the Jewish community because of the similarity between the Greek root *holo* and the Hebrew word *olah*.
7. Isaiah 47:11: "Therefore shall evil come upon thee, thou shalt not know from whence it riseth; and mischief shall fall upon thee, thou shalt not be able to put it off; and *desolation* shall come upon thee suddenly, which thou shalt not know."
8. It occurs six times in all in the Bible: once in the Book of Isaiah, once in Psalms (35:8), three times in Job (30:3, 30:14 and 38:27) and once in Zephaniah (1:15).
9. So much so that people asked him, "Was it you who made the *Shoah*?" To which he replied, "No, it was Hitler who made the Shoah; I made *Shoah*."
10. Chicago, Quadrangle Books, 1961.

3. The question of representation

The Nazis did their utmost to prevent representation of their atrocities: window dressing, faked photos and propaganda films spread a "soft" image of the camps. It was therefore important to use other, more truthful, images to re-establish the truth. But these images appeared so traumatising that they provoked controversy aimed at limiting their dissemination, demonstrating to what extent representation of the Shoah could be problematic. Certain books[11] have taken stock of this delicate matter. They show that, because of these inescapable images, the modern consciousness has turned the Nazi genocide into a prism through which to view the rest of society, an unavoidable benchmark for all modern and historical acts of political violence, and a perspective that determines the way victims of any origin must appear. This public awareness inevitably tends to make evil banal, since it concurrently produces a popular terminology (holocaust, camp, etc.), an intertextuality which turns images of trains or mass graves into recurrent metaphors or metonymies, and a wholesale reduction of reality to omnipresent stereotypes. This is now "the truth of an aesthetics of representation which can now only operate in self-referential modes governed by code systems".[12] At its origin is a fairly conventional process: the fact that there is little or no raw archival material encourages approximation and inevitably entails a tendency towards instrumentalisation, reification and conferral of a kind of sacred status, which arises from a refusal or inability to grieve. As a result, the genocide of the Jews acquires a dimension impossible to represent and becomes more inaccessible than ever, thus adding to the various moral and theological barriers that already exist:

– "Thou shalt not make unto thee any graven image". This commandment from the Torah, which is to be found in Exodus (20:4-6), Leviticus (26:1) and Deuteronomy (4:15-18), prohibits Jews from making images. This precaution against idolatry actually goes beyond invented images, since it includes natural images, such as those of the planets, for example. This original prohibition has undoubtedly weighed heavy on Jewish painting, sculpture and cinema;[13]

– To this original prohibition is added, as far as the Shoah is concerned, the perfectly understandable repugnance of survivors who cannot bear to see the reality which they lived through become an object of entertainment;

– The third barrier to representation arises from the fact that since a punctilious cinematic morality has decreed the Shoah to be unrepresentable, anything which represents it has been described as obscene. The Nazi aim of reducing everything to ashes in order to leave no trace has created an absence making it impossible to

---

11. Judith E. Doneson, *The Holocaust in American Film*, Syracuse University Press, 2001; and Philippe Mesnard, id., *Consciences de la Shoah*, Kimé, 2000.
12. Mesnard, id., p. 39.
13. See Alain Besançon, *L'image interdite*, Gallimard, *Folio essais*, 2000. However, the Bible describes moving images in the first Solomon's Temple.

see what actually happened. It produced a material disablement that paralysed us. This invisible crime renders any visual reconstruction questionable;

– Last but not least, television productions are achieved in order to stir superficial and fleeting pseudo-emotions unworthy of an event of this magnitude.

Imre Kertész said that "it is impossible to film the Shoah". He insisted on writing the screenplay for the adaptation of his novel *Fateless* by the film-maker Lajos Koltai in order to ensure that the film would remain faithful to the text. From the very first films on the subject, cinematic representation has indeed been the subject of lengthy controversy. The debate was opened by the original review of Gillo Pontecorvo's film *Kapo* (1960) by Jacques Rivette in *Cahiers du cinéma*. The article, entitled "De l'abjection", specifically condemned the final tracking shot, which crudely laboured the wholesale murder of the prisoners.[14] This debate laid the foundations for a critical relationship to entertainment based on what could or could not be shown. For the Shoah is the ultimate in terror: any portrayal would seem only to relativise or trivialise it. This was what Elie Wiesel wrote when the *Holocaust* television mini-series was broadcast.[15] The idea worried Stanley Kubrick when he was planning his film on this subject entitled *The Aryan Papers* and, according to his wife, explains his abandonment of the project just as much as the purely commercial fact that Spielberg had begun making *Schindler's List*. Another controversy about cinematic representation of the Shoah was initiated by Claude Lanzmann, who felt that he had done the only acceptable thing: interviewing eyewitnesses who recount in words, without any flashbacks, the crucial experience they went through – witnesses immediately involved in the genocide as victims, perpetrators or unwilling underlings. Jean-Luc Godard supported him and emphasised cinema's great failure in this field. These arguments can be applied to any film endeavouring to represent a crime against humanity.

As is apparent, the matter is complex and impossible to untangle other than by studying the key films that have been the landmarks and bones of contention in this discussion, which is more topical than ever. Two important books have already dealt with the subject of representing the Shoah: *Indelible Shadows: Film and the Holocaust* by Annette Insdorf, first published in the United States[16] and reissued in France in 1985, and *The Holocaust in American Film*[17] by Judith E. Doneson, which confined itself to American cinema. However, new films come

---

14. "Look, however, in *Kapo* at the shot where [Emmanuelle] Riva commits suicide by throwing herself on the electrified barbed wire: a man who decides, at this moment, to dolly in so as to reframe the body in a low-angle shot, taking care to put the raised hand precisely in one corner of the final shot, deserves nothing but the profoundest contempt" (*Cahiers du cinéma*, No. 120, June 1961). In fact, it is not so much the tracking shot that Rivette is censuring as the way in which it finishes, with the close-up, low-angle shot reframing Emmanuelle Riva's face and thus crudely victimising her. Rivette's moralising position was subsequently much disputed.
15. "The Trivializing of the Holocaust: semi-fact and semi-fiction", *New York Times*, 16 April 1978.
16. Random House, 1983. A third edition (published by Cambridge University Press) came out in 2003.
17. Op. cit.

out every year. We shall try to deal with world cinema past and present, admittedly without any claim to exhaustiveness but selecting films that are emblematic of certain trends. We shall thus endeavour to go beyond that "fundamentalism" which has turned the Shoah into a religious absolute as impossible to represent as God himself. Should we really be as pessimistic as Godard on the cinema's ability to address these taboo subjects? Before answering this question, some theoretical, moral and aesthetic preliminaries are necessary.

4. Cinema and history

History with a capital "h" is one of cinema's favourite subjects. From its very beginnings, cinema understood the importance of historical reconstruction in terms of both record and entertainment. But above all, while it "appears to reproduce and reflect a certain vision of the world" through the types of behaviours and values that characterise the society that it chooses as background, cinema "aims to create a specific point of view".[18] Past events will be represented differently depending on the period, the director's opinions and the target audience. The Shoah is no exception to this rule. The specific problem raised by historical cinema is that it is not content to depict well-known and pre-digested events. In fact, as Pierre Sorlin has demonstrated,[19] historical films are as much about the present in which they are made as about the past which they depict. Thus, by pointing up America's guilt with respect to the Jewish genocide, *Judgment at Nuremberg* also functions as a metaphor for the history of the 1960s, recalling both National Socialism and McCarthyism. Memory is a two-edged sword. But the second problem that it raises is "how to remember without propagating and how to perpetuate without perpetrating",[20] that is, how to maintain the necessary distance in relation to the events related. For all these reasons, cinema must be treated as an art rather than a history book. And "art never commemorates. Its role is not to remember [...] If art, in general, is concerned with memory it is with the strange memory of something that has never been lodged in specific recollections and that therefore cannot be either forgotten or remembered, since we have never known or experienced it, and yet it never deserts us".[21] Cinema works by using not only the actual facts but also obsessions and collective guilt.

The Shoah is a historical event for which we have some archival film material, Nazi propaganda films, and footage shot by the Allies during the liberation of the

---

18. Dominique Chansel, *Europe on-screen: Cinema and the teaching of history*, Council of Europe Publishing, 2001.
19. "La Shoah: une représentation impossible?", in *Les institutions de l'image*, edited by Jean-Pierre Bertin-Maghit and Béatrice Fleury-Vilate, with a preface by Marc Ferro, Éditions de l'École des Hautes Études en Sciences Sociales, 2001.
20. Eliette Abécassis, "Peut-on parler de la Shoah?", *Le Nouvel Observateur*, special issue, *La mémoire de la Shoah*, December 2003/January 2004.
21. Jean-Luc Nancy, "L'immémorial", in *Art, mémoire, commémoration*, Éditions Voix Richard Meyer/École Nationale Supérieure d'Art de Nancy, 1999.

camps. Sylvie Lindeperg[22] has studied the genealogy of British footage of liberation of the camps, revealing how different layers of reception have accumulated. These pieces of visual evidence, haunted by the fear of rebuttal, have become a sort of raw material for other films (documentary and fiction) and have ended up an integral part of the imagery of the destruction of the European Jews. Verisimilitude is now created by an impression of *déjà vu,* which appeals more to the imagination than to the eye. Every film about the Shoah takes into account this initial material. But how was this material itself produced?

It was the need to supply evidence that led Sidney Bernstein, who headed the Film Section of the Psychological Warfare Division of SHAEF (Supreme Headquarters Allied Expeditionary Force), to arrange for a systematic film record of everything the British army discovered. The commissioned film, *Memory of the Camps,* dating from 1945, raises for the first time the basic questions of how to make a coherent film out of disparate elements and how to render this film authentic. It was the director Alfred Hitchcock who, called in to help, found the answers to these technical problems. He employed establishing shots that were as wide as possible and generalised the use of pans in order to discourage any suspicion of faking. This film, consisting of archival footage and oral accounts and meant to be both memorial and testimony, consequently goes further than the problem of credibility to raise that of irrefutability.[23] It records horrific spectacles, accumulates evidence, draws out witnesses and shows images. But in doing so it raises a much thornier moral problem, which continued to crop up subsequently, namely "the impact of rhetoric on instruments of proof in history".[24] By rejecting a *mise en scène* in this specific case, Hitchcock immediately declares such a *mise en scène* to be impossible, improper and obscene. But a film cannot exist without staging, and this rejection itself is a *mise en scène.* Even shots which are powerful in their own right are subject to this law. The *mise en scène* probably represents the distance needed by the film-maker to avoid being fascinated by the violence or the pathos.

In the light of these premises regarding their historical value, how are we to define films about the Shoah? The concept is extremely broad. Like Judith E. Doneson,[25] I would say that it covers all the films representing one of the stages of the process described by Raul Hilberg, from the April 1933 laws in Germany prohibiting Jews from public employment, up to the liberation, in 1945, of the last concentration camps. To these I shall add films dealing with the consequences of the Shoah up to the present for survivors, descendants and those directly or indirectly responsible. These films may be either documentary or fiction.

22. At the Council of Europe symposium on *Teaching about the Holocaust and Artistic Creation,* 15-18 October 2002.
23. See Martine Joly, "Le cinéma d'archives, preuve de l'histoire?", *Les Institutions de l'image,* op. cit.
24. Paul Ricoeur, "Philosophies de l'histoire: recherche, explication, écriture", in *Philosophical Problems Today,* Guttorm Floistad (ed.), cited by Martine Joly, op. cit.
25. Op. cit., p. 6.

5. Documentary and fiction

The difference between documentary and fiction, so firmly fixed in the viewer's system of representation, vanishes upon closer study. Cinema is commonly identified with narration. It tells stories. This paradox, which brings with it the requirement for both fiction and credibility, has led to countless misunderstandings. On the one hand, the audience fails to recognise the non-narrative elements that enter into any film story, and on the other it is unaware of the underlying narrative nature of any documentary. "Documentary is what happens to others, and fiction is what happens to me," Godard once said, echoing an incisive remark by Sartre: "The adventure only begins when you start to relate it." Is not a narrative by definition something that turns everyday experience into an adventure and real life into fiction? In the point of view adopted, its minor distortions of an elusive truth and emphasis on specific aspects, any narrative may be regarded as both a documentary and a work of imagination. Cinema has played on this duality from the outset. Immediately caught between two apparently conflicting temptations – encouraging belief in the reality of the representation and encouraging acceptance of a fictional world that does away with the real – it played with the credulity of a completely new audience. Spectators who were very different from theatregoers and able to forget the device by which they were being manipulated surrendered themselves completely to the irrational terror or delight offered by this new type of entertainment. Has enough really been written about the fear and violent reactions of cinema audiences in the early days, helpless in the face of the pitfalls of identification?[26] It subsequently became customary to draw an arbitrary but convenient distinction between documentary and fiction cinema. This dividing line, still very much present in the minds of today's cinemagoers, represents a purely conventional boundary, which is blurred and tenuous, since "everything that marks cinema out for a documentary vocation is not enough to cancel out that greater symbolism which has created it out of a world abandoned to the vertigo of the imagination".[27] What Jean-Louis Comolli calls "true registration" (*inscription vraie*) is the fact that the camera's unique eye will never be able to register what is in front of it in the same way as our senses; film, however documentary in nature, will always be different both from what has been perceived and from what has been intended by the film-maker. It is Sartre again who, in his *Critique of Dialectical Reason*, stresses this fundamental difference between the project and its implementation, the dream and its realisation. But, in addition, cinemagoers are prey to a delusion that makes them believe that the performance is more true than the reality, believe in the characters, believe what the characters believe, and

---

26. Even if the famous fright caused by the Lumière brothers' film of a train pulling into a station has already been amply exaggerated and publicised so as to become a legend.
27. "Éloge du ciné-monstre", Jean-Louis Comolli, *Cinéma du Réel* Festival Catalogue, 1995, p. 48.

so on, in an infinite whirl.[28] This specularity of the "imaginary signifier"[29] is the secret of its success. Over time, film-makers have repeatedly given new impetus to the desire for fiction, endlessly playing with the power of representation, both creating and undermining belief, and whittling away the boundary between reality and illusion.

This basic ambiguity has rendered increasingly inadequate the boundary between fiction, based on imaginary characters and a plot, and documentary, in which real people involved in fascinating human adventures take on an archetypal aspect. A documentary may consist of archival material, eyewitness accounts, slices of life, etc. However, the treatment of space and time differs between the genres, even if real time has been taken over for fiction by demanding film-makers such as Chantal Akerman. Laying siege to symbolic spaces and not hesitating to cover extensive periods, documentary cinema thus conveys a particularly keen sense of reality.

Yet while the documentary is considered worthy of dealing with the Shoah, as Claude Lanzmann and Alain Resnais have demonstrated, the fiction film, for its part, is suspected of triviality, and all the more so if it does not employ a staunch arsenal of realist weapons and treat the historical reality as sacred. But all films, we now know, are fiction, whose impression of reality is built on the coherence of the narrative world they establish. Documentaries are no less narrative, artificial or "frivolous" than fiction films. They often contain nothing spontaneous, immediate, or even taken from life. Figures are often posed, and the choice of static, frontal or sideways tracking shot is always a choice of *mise en scène*.

As for the degree of credibility implied by a film depending on the genre to which it belongs, this must always be carefully specified in order to prevent the viewer from accepting uncritically the story portrayed on screen.

Archival footage is not historical reconstruction, and the latter is separate from eyewitness accounts, while, in the field of narration, a faithful portrayal of history is far removed from a fable, tale or pastiche. The average cinemagoer does not make a clear distinction between genres, as shown by the controversy surrounding Roberto Benigni's film *Life Is Beautiful*, which has been criticised for its inaccuracy although it claims to be a "fable". It is therefore always necessary to provide very specific clarification of this point.

---

28. This is the denial effect described by psychoanalysis: "I know it's not true, but I believe it just the same."

29. The title of an essay by Christian Metz, translated by Celia Britton, Annwyl Williams, Ben Brewster and Alfred Guzzetti: *The Imaginary Signifier: Psychoanalysis and the Cinema*, Indiana University Press, 1982.

6. Overstatement and understatement

The point here is to understand the issues in the controversies to which these films have given rise. It seems that inexperienced cinemagoers expect the cinema to provide them with information which they require to be reliable. Because of the realism of moving images, they believe as firmly in what they see on the large screen as what they see on television, hear on the radio or read in their papers. The image is deemed to be authentic, even if it has begun to be suspect since the so-called Timisoara massacre – the video footage of which has permanently shaken the trust of some television viewers – and since computer manipulation of digital photos has been within everyone's reach.

Furthermore, such cinemagoers, fed on strong emotions by television, which does not hold back on footage of slaughter, are large-scale consumers of emotional information. Sitting in front of their televisions they are permanently receptive to partisan passions and ready to rally to the grand political or humanitarian causes plugged by political parties and various "telethons", whether these causes are national or international. To encourage them, television makes ample use of overstatement. Shamelessly emphasising the pathos of the most critical situations and aiming for dramatic effect, it appeals, like melodrama, to basic emotions, often with insidious intent, with the aim of provoking indignation, outrage, disgust and tears. To this end, anything will do. Mass manipulation can thus pass unnoticed. Such overstatement has deep-seated causes. At the symposium on teaching the Shoah held in Strasbourg by the Council of Europe (in October 2002), the philosopher Marie-Josée Mondzain emphasised that, since the Shoah, art and culture have been marked by forms of psychological release, violence and hallucination, as if the Shoah had removed all censorship of the most barbarous of fantasies. This is a blatant collapse of symbolism, which expresses itself in the negation of all taboos. Daily we see on our screens (large and small) the invasion of this new visual totalitarianism that wants to show everything, appealing to a most depraved sense of pleasure and unscrupulously eroticising violence. Similarly, for Ernst Cassirer, the culture of murder could only spring from the murder of culture, and violence in a culture gives rise to a culture of violence. Only the symbol, that specifically human gift, can enable us to break out of this vicious circle. We may therefore legitimately enquire after the use of symbols today and consider that they should be urgently restored. This is the role of art, which must take on this infringement of freedom and face the challenge that consists in recounting, more symbolically than narratively, an event which negates all means of expression and makes any images impossible in the same way as a theological prohibition. It is on how it meets this challenge that it must be judged.

Understatement, on the other hand, is a stylistic device in literature, defined for the cinema by Alfred Hitchcock when François Truffaut was interviewing him about his film *The Trouble with Harry*.[30] It consists in saying little to suggest a great deal,

---

30. In François Truffaut's book, *Hitchcock*, Simon & Schuster, 1985.

expressing all emotions with restraint, toning down all effects and rejecting tragedy and pathos. This is the speciality of humour, which arises from the asymmetry between signifier and the signified, and between the method of expression and the reality expressed, with systematic underrating of serious events while exaggerating the insignificant to the point of scandal. Thus, depending on which of these two tendencies is chosen, cinema writing can be either overelaborate, insistent and even redundant, or else restrained and concentrated, playing with ellipsis and letting the viewer's imagination do its work. There is a gulf between these two approaches, which have had varying fortunes.

7. Realism and anti-realism

As far as representation of the Shoah or any other crime against humanity is concerned, the choice between realistic representation and antirealism is as much moral as aesthetic: moral because, even for the purpose of drawing attention to the fact, it is immoral to insist too complacently on the suffering of others. This was the cinematic ethic of Rivette, who turned each aesthetic decision into a moral choice. As for Godard, he believes that "a tracking shot is a moral issue". Admittedly, realism in cinema is the result of certain conventions. An impression of reality can be produced by a few details and simple allusions without requiring laboured effects or a meticulous depiction of reality. Realism is an artificial effect bearing no relation to reality itself – an effect associated with an entire body of films in the same genre or on the same subject. Ellipsis, a basic element of cinematic grammar, and of artistic expression in general, makes it possible not to have to reconstruct in minute detail the actual places or period being represented or to stage piles of bodies, even if the real bodies had such an impact on the people who saw the first documentaries. It may be added that this type of footage today makes no impression on indifferent audiences who have been living on a diet of blood as a result of the fashion for gore films.[31] Benigni has shown that it is more effective to make the viewers themselves conjure up such images, which now form part of our collective unconscious. To dwell on them would be not only immoral and, as it were, obscene (obscenity consisting in a sensual or shocking object being displayed complacently for some advantage), but also pointless.

The other arts have realised this. The detached tone adopted by Primo Levi, Imre Kertész and Wladyslaw Szpilman to recount their memories of the camps or the ghetto is far more moving. The linear narrative and their technique of inner focus recreate their emotions more effectively than any images. The same has always been true of sculpture and painting. According to Pliny the Elder, when the Greek painter Timanthes painted *The Sacrifice of Iphigenia* he veiled Agamemnon's face, considering it immodest to represent his expression. The famous statue of Laocoon, today in the Belvedere Palace in Rome, has its mouth half-open as if it were

---

31. The gore genre consists of films that show phenomena which, by their violent or bloody nature, are designed to arouse revulsion and loathing in the audience.

forbidden to show the hero screaming. Moreover, in his *Laocoon* Lessing wrote that an artist has only one choice – to soften the expression of suffering or hide it completely – if he wishes to stir emotion whilst respecting the laws of aesthetics. Many theorists of the Renaissance and of Mannerism advised a similar approach for representing the Passion of Christ, a subject much debated between Gothic artists, who endeavoured to portray his suffering realistically, and Romanesque artists, who preferred to depict him in majesty. Their choices were always theological, aesthetic and moral. Nevertheless, painters such as Leonardo da Vinci exhorted the artist's gaze to be pitiless, so as to cause terror, and believed that this *terribiltà* had a provocative beauty. Later artists such as Géricault, Goya and Schiele chose realism and even expressionism as the most effective means of revealing human suffering or protesting against oppression, but art theorists have always thought that even if art has every privilege, there should be certain limits to representation. And sex and death, so cheapened today, have always been the two taboos that have imposed such limits, since, in art, imagination plays the main role.

And all the more so in cinema, where ellipsis plays a key part. Some people say that the absence of gas-chamber images in a film encourages denial of their reality. But we may reply, firstly, that denial is a state of mind which does not require evidence and that the images themselves can no longer be regarded as reliable now that we know how easy it is to manipulate them and introduce special effects, and, secondly, that cinema is not simply a medium like television but rather an art, and actually one of the major arts of our time. It must therefore respect the same rules as the other arts. And each of the arts is perhaps better able to give an account of reality using its own means of expression than is the archival material itself. In his book *Literature or Life* Jorge Semprun indeed shows that it is impossible to give people an idea of the smell of death that hung over the camps other than through literature. This is also what the painter Zoran Music shows by painting indefinable shadows, more dreadful than photographs of real corpses. But such a position meets with less and less understanding nowadays when Hollywood provides the dominant model of cinema, which is not one of expressionism but rather of the most fulsome overstatement. It is only as art that the cinema is worthy and able to deal with the Shoah, and it is as art that it must be presented to students. It therefore seems increasingly necessary to associate the teaching of history with the teaching of art history and to explain how films should be viewed before cinema can be used properly and judiciously to perpetuate the memory of the Shoah.

8. Filmic and profilmic codes

The problem raised by cinematic representation of the Shoah and crimes against humanity in general is that of conveying an event which defies visual and verbal expression through a favoured form which, of all the media, undoubtedly makes the greatest use of codes. For the image, it must be clearly stated and understood, is never neutral. In her book *Indelible Shadows*, Annette Insdorf raises the major question of "how certain cinematic devices express or evade the moral issues inherent in the subject", that is, the form given by each film to the reality conveyed. We should actually go further and raise the more general issue of the function of images and the role of film in the production system of a given period or society. Veit Harlan's *Jew Süss* can be understood only in the propaganda climate of 1940s Germany, and the sentimental tendency of Hollywood cinema explains the characters in *Holocaust*. Once again, historical films tell us as much about the present as about the past.

Let us try at least to give an idea of the codes that come into play in the production of a film. Profilmic codes is the name given to all codes whose choice precedes the actual making of the film – choice of setting, choice of genre (historical reconstruction, updating or stylisation), casting, etc. – while filmic codes relate to the specific language of cinema. They concern the narration proper, its order and chronology, and the structure of the screenplay, which will depend on whether a partial or exhaustive account of events is chosen, whether it starts at the beginning or the end, and whether it is linear or jumps around in time. They also cover camera movements, the framing and scale of shots, and the choice of colour. Although they are at the director's discretion, these choices are not purely individual and aesthetic: they presuppose a point of view concerning the story and history, a willingness to subscribe to some theories rather than others, and the aim of promoting the theory chosen with varying degrees of vigour. For all films are supported by a set of arguments. These codes are therefore ideological and deliberately guide the audience's view. It is only by pointing out their existence and the constraints which they introduce that we can highlight and possibly neutralise their effects. There is thus one stylistic feature that recurs almost systematically in these films, from *Night and Fog* to *Schindler's List*: the combination of black-and-white and colour, with colour being used for the present day and black-and-white for flashbacks in the camps, as if it were archival material, which is not always the case. If we are to understand the issues involved, we must ask why this recurrent choice is made.[32]

9. The question of comedy

The status of comedy must also be clarified. Benigni's choice of comedy has been considered unpardonable sacrilege. And yet ... have we forgotten Lubitsch's *To Be or Not to Be* or Chaplin's *The Great Dictator*? Is not Alfred Jarry's *Ubu Roi* one of the sternest denunciations of dictatorship? The suspicion hanging over comedy probably stems from public ignorance. Yet Plato has already analysed the "combinations of pleasure and pain in lamentations, and in tragedy and comedy, not only on the stage, but on the greater stage of human life".[33] And throughout

---

32. Black-and-white has always been regarded as a mark of cinematic realism, despite all attempts to make it less natural, as if its different degrees of intensity formed not two colours but only one, the fabric of the film and consequently that of the referent itself and in particular of the past. See the entries on *Night and Fog*, *Sophie's Choice* and *Schindler's List*.
33. *Philebus*, translation by Benjamin Jowett.

history, comedy has been regarded as better able than serious genres to "correct morals through laughter", as witnessed Molière and Voltaire. *Candide* undoubtedly constitutes the most effective challenge ever made to war and the slaughter it occasions. Moreover, a whole range of gradations is possible in comedy, from the crude effects of burlesque, farce and slapstick to humour and irony which play with understatement, innuendo and antiphrasis. Overstatement and understatement again. Furthermore, when power is deified, laughter becomes blasphemy and political comedy anathema.

The suffering of survivors of the Nazi camps, like the suffering of any victims who survive crimes against humanity, must be supremely respected. So why should that suffering prohibit representation of the Shoah on screen? Is it because cinema is considered too "frivolous" a medium? And why not resort to comedy in cinema and theatre to expose the horror and absurdity of a totalitarian system and its most vicious frenzies? This prejudice would seem to disregard the corrosive force of comedy and its critical and subversive value as well as to overlook the fact that humour is the secret weapon of the oppressed everywhere. Instead of dismissing a particular genre or form outright, without attempting to analyse it, it would be better to measure its effectiveness or power. Many viewers, shocked by extremely harsh images of the camps, which offend their sensibilities, can be moved by less dramatic images which, without misrepresenting the history of the Shoah, can recount it unobtrusively in the form of satire or caricature. People come out of *Life Is Beautiful* with tears in their eyes. At no point is Benigni lacking in respect for victims of Nazism. Neither Chaplin nor Lubitsch underestimated the risks – on the contrary. Their humour was one of despair, rediscovering the very essence of Jewish humour.

If we dismiss it out of hand and distort their intentions, we are in danger of understanding nothing at all.

Conclusion

With this clarification in mind, it becomes possible to show a film to students while stressing such and such an element, depending on the film, and to initiate a discussion that will not waste time and energy. The cinematic framework has been established, and we can address the actual subject of the Shoah, its history and its victims, taking care to explain that the Shoah is more than just a historical truth, having become the very symbol of horror in modern times. This is why it is referred to as a benchmark for any collective crimes still being committed. However, art works with symbols. In former times, were Goya and Hieronymus Bosch denied the right to represent – symbolically and non-anecdotally, in a minimalistic or expressionistic and often caricatural style – the atrocities that they had experienced? Cinema has today come to occupy a position comparable to that of painting. It is perfectly legitimate for this major modern art form to deal with all the tragedies of our time without its images being suspected of systematically minimising, watering down or disguising reality. On the contrary, "our time seems to have grasped the dangers of showing barbarous images indiscriminately".[34] It can manifest discretion in its representations of barbarity and avoid the misuse of rhetoric. We therefore need have no fear of seeing the Shoah or other crimes against humanity "trivialised" or "vulgarised" by the cinema, by fiction or by comedy. "Silence alone is deadly".[35] The more these crimes are represented, the more certain they are to remain in the collective memory as so much evidence of the regression of a civilisation which thought itself advanced and which has lost this illusion. Admittedly, television provides an introduction to cinema, both fictional and documentary; it can support film libraries and film societies in their task of publicising history and the literary and theatrical heritage, and it has done much for global knowledge of the Shoah, as the *Holocaust* mini-series demonstrates. It is therefore a key teaching aid. But cinema is an art form and should be included in the curriculum by introducing younger generations to its techniques as soon as possible so that they do not run the risk of misinterpreting film images.

---

34. Vicente Sanchez-Biosca, "Représenter l'irreprésentable", *Les Institutions de l'image*, op. cit.
35. Jean-Philippe Guérand, "Chaplin, Lewis, Benigni: rire de la Shoah", *Le Nouvel Observateur*, special issue No. 53, December 2003/January 2004.

PART ONE
DOCUMENTARY VIEWS

A. One school of thought

1. Pioneers

Alain Resnais, *Nuit et brouillard (Night and Fog)*

France (1955), 32 min.; language: French; commentary: Jean Cayrol

Historical theme: systematic elimination of opponents of Nazism

Moral theme: denunciation of a collective crime

Aesthetic themes: rejection of historical reconstruction, status of archival material, gap between past and present, ellipsis, antithesis

The director

Born in 1922, Alain Resnais started making films at the age of 14 with an 8 mm camera, and in 1943 enrolled at the French film school – the Institut des Hautes Études Cinématographiques (IDHEC) – in the editing department. He began his career by shooting a number of short films on art subjects such as *Van Gogh* (1948) and *Guernica* (1950). But it was his documentary about the Nazi camps, *Night and Fog* (1955), which made his reputation. Early on in the New Wave, his first full-length film, *Hiroshima mon amour* (1959), revolutionised classic narrative technique, trying out the ideas of playing with memory and destructuring the narrative which he took further in *Last Year at Marienbad* (1961) and which were to engross him right up to *Life is a Bed of Roses* (1983). As he is a committed film-maker, the themes of war and politics are also very much present in his work (*Muriel*, 1963; *Stavisky*, 1974). Alain Resnais has often worked with writers such as Marguerite Duras and Alain Robbe-Grillet for his scripts. In 1992 he made *Smoking/No Smoking* with Jean-Pierre Bacri and Agnès Jaoui, and in 1997 he had a great popular success with *Same Old Song*.

The film

1. Cast

Narrator: Michel Bouquet

2. Background

In 1955, at the request of the French Committee for the History of the Second World War, Alain Resnais visited the sites where thousands of men, women and children had lost their lives: Oranienburg, Auschwitz, Dachau, Ravensbruck, Belsen, Neuengamme and Struthof. With Jean Cayrol and the help of archival material, he recalls the slow martyrdom of the inmates.

The documentary is named after Hitler's *Nacht und Nebel (Night and Fog)* programme, which itself takes its name from German mythology, revisited by Wagner.[36] Hitler used this expression to refer to the programme for rounding up opponents of the regime and making them disappear without trace. On 7 December 1941 Hitler published the Nacht und Nebel Decree, which replaced the ineffective Nazi policy of taking hostages to counter underground activities. Suspected underground agents and others would now vanish without trace into the night and fog. SS Reichsführer Himmler issued the following instructions to the Gestapo: "After lengthy consideration, it is the will of the Führer that the measures taken against those who are guilty of offences against the Reich or against the occupation forces in occupied areas should be altered. The Führer is of the opinion that in such cases penal servitude or even a hard labour sentence for life will be regarded as a sign of weakness. An effective and lasting deterrent can be achieved only by the death penalty or by taking measures which will leave the family and the population uncertain as to the fate of the offender. Deportation to Germany serves this purpose." Field Marshal Keitel issued a letter stating: "Efficient and enduring intimidation can only be achieved either by capital punishment or by measures by which the relatives of the criminals do not know the fate of the criminal [...] The prisoners are, in future, to be transported to Germany secretly, and further treatment of the offenders will take place here; these measures will have a deterrent effect because: *a.* the prisoners will vanish without a trace, *b.* no information may be given to their relations as to their whereabouts or their fate."[37]

3. Analysis

The film opens with a long tracking shot of a peaceful landscape in colour, while Jean Cayrol's commentary, spoken by Michel Bouquet, introduces the impassive façade of Auschwitz against a background of lyrical music by Hans Eisler, immediately creating the first of the counterpoints meant to startle, with the background music becoming increasingly incongruous and out of place as the shots plunge deeper into the horror of the past. Other contrasts are introduced between stasis and movement, colour and black-and-white, hope and despair, memory and oblivion. With clips from newsreel footage of the time, silent material, and genuine or spurious archival footage (the problem here is that Resnais used as archival footage excerpts from the fiction film *The Last Stage*, shot by Wanda Jakubowska, an Auschwitz inmate, shortly after her liberation), as well as brutal images of sealed trains and barbed-wire fences, the camera explores the camp to the limits of suggestion, pausing occasionally on a static shot. A balance is

---

36. The character of Alberich the Nibelung in *Rheingold* was able, by putting on his magic helmet, to turn into a cloud of smoke with the incantation: "Night and fog, visible to no one."
37. www.belgiumww2.info

achieved between the unbearable images, the elliptical commentary spoken in a perfectly restrained monotone, and the delicate music, by allowing the images to speak for themselves. Photographs take the place of footage as if marking with their fixedness an indelible trace of what has disappeared. The alternation of peaceful present and agonising past prompts us to ask some key questions: Who was responsible? Is it possible to obliterate all trace of such crimes completely? Are they actually credible? Such is the lesson of this "cubist" film, which pieces together reality after having shattered it but which never waters it down.

4. Teaching suggestions

Comment in particular on the colour shots of the bare Auschwitz landscape and the director's use of contrasts to show how even a documentary film such as this one is dependent on an aesthetics that has to be decoded. The brutality of some of the other images needs no comment. But it should nevertheless be pointed out that the film has dated for a number of reasons:

– it fails to distinguish between concentration camps and extermination camps;

– it bolsters the idea that the Nazis manufactured soap from human fat, which subsequently proved not to have been pursued beyond the experimental stage;

– it draws no distinctions between victims, making only one, seemingly fortuitous, reference to "a Jewish student";

– it does not explain that the famous bulldozers moving dead bodies were driven by British soldiers, who were obliged to bury the dead quickly to prevent epidemics;

– lastly, intervention by the censors led to the cutting of a sequence showing a French gendarme on duty at the Pithiviers camp.

Re-establishing the truth does not in any way detract from the film's effectiveness.

Marcel Ophüls, *Le chagrin et la pitié, chronique d'une ville française sous l'Occupation (The Sorrow and the Pity, Chronicle of a French City under the Occupation)*

France/Switzerland/West Germany (1970), 265 min.; languages: French, German, English

Historical theme: French collaboration in the systematic destruction of the Jews

Moral theme: fear as a corrupter of humanity

Aesthetic themes: rejection of historical reconstruction, eyewitness accounts, gap between past and present

The director

Marcel Ophüls, born in Frankfurt-am-Main in 1927, is the son of the great German director Max Ophüls. After a sketch in the film *Love at Twenty* in 1961 and an interesting X-rated film *Banana Peel*, he created a scandal in 1971 with *The Sorrow and the Pity*, rejected by television until 1981, which brought him accusations of being anti-Gaullist. To these the film-maker replied: "It is only anti-Gaullist inasmuch as it disputes the myth of French greatness [...] It offers a different perception of history [...] which is based on individual behaviour and asks questions about collective memory" (*Le Monde*, 18 August 1981). A committed film-maker par excellence, he subsequently made in France *Hotel Terminus*, a biographical film about Klaus Barbie, and *The Troubles We've Seen: A History of Journalism in Wartime*, and, in Germany, *The Memory of Justice* (1976) and *November Days* (1991).

The film

1. Cast

Script and interviews: Marcel Ophüls and André Harris

Producers: André Harris and Alain de Sedouy

Interviewees: politicians such as Pierre Mendès France, Jacques Duclos and Anthony Eden, soldiers, Nazi dignitaries, Resistance fighters, shopkeepers, the Comte de Chambrun (Laval's son-in-law), and a Frenchman who joined a division of the Waffen SS

2. Background

Marcel Ophüls wanted to chronicle life in a French city under the Occupation. He chose Clermont-Ferrand as an emblematic place capable of revealing the history of the period, given that it was occupied, supported Pétain and was also a hub of the Resistance, constituting one of the points of a symbolic triangle in the Auvergne, the other two being Vichy and Gergovie. It thus provides a perfect illustration of the complexity of the actual situation in France. The director has produced four and a half hours of kaleidoscopic intercutting of various material – interviews, newsreel, photos and speeches – whose coherence gradually becomes apparent.

3. Analysis

By mixing period newsreel – French, German and British – with interviews with various players in the tragedy, the director is trying to convey the knotty complexity of a confused period repressed by the collective unconsciousness – that of Vichy France – and gauge its consequences in 1969. Ophüls' intention is not to reconstruct what happened during the war but rather to show "what was shown to people during the war". He lets us listen to Nazi and French propaganda and has thus produced, through eyewitnesses' recollections and silences, a lively oral history enabling us to reconnect with the human context.

Fragmentation is pursued here through exceptionally inventive editing, and if each interview is broken up, this is in order to reveal a range of reactions on each subject covered, from collaboration to the Resistance. Claude Vajda's editing therefore has a dramatic and heuristic role, since it brings out the stark contrasts between conflicting assertions and contradictory accounts.

By thus interviewing eyewitnesses of all opinions, Ophüls introduced a method that was subsequently to be used by Claude Lanzmann: witnesses are filmed in their home or work environment like ordinary people, and the interviewer is apparent only through skilfully directed questions and subtle visual details. There are, however, some exceptions to this principle of non-intervention: when Ophüls loses his temper and contradicts Chambrun, when he announces the Vélodrome d'Hiver round-up in a voice-over, and when he avoids breaking up the interview with Claude Lévy. The object is to demonstrate that collaborators were not monsters but rather fearful manipulated beings, living on their guard and fiercely defending their minor privileges. A lack of communication, mutual distrust, prejudice, paternalism and a selfish preference for a quiet life doubtless explain the birth of Pétainism, fear being perhaps the strongest motive. Ophüls also analyses Nazi propaganda (which laid emphasis on the disorderliness of the French troops and the prestige of the German army, with its impeccable organisation) and stereotyping in French and German newsreels and in excerpts from Veit Harlan's film *Jew Süss*. The director thus manages to establish the need to link everyday life with a political conscience. This is indeed cinema designed to awaken the viewer's critical faculties.

4. Teaching suggestions

It is worth making the director's approach clear by showing the class one or two sequences and asking what the film-maker's motives are for departing from his principles, which facts the witnesses are trying to hide, and what their degree of involvement is in the episode that they are recounting. It will be seen, for example, how the Comte de Chambrun tries to exculpate Laval, his father-in-law, while Dr Claude Lévy discloses that Laval offered four thousand Jewish children to the Germans without being asked.

It should also be explained why the general public – for whom the cinema had drawn a veil over Vichy and collaboration, keeping only proud images relating to the Resistance – refused to recognise itself in this page of its own history. *"The Sorrow and the Pity* reminded the French of what had actually happened during this period: how France had crumbled under the inexorable advance of German power; how the Vichy government had thought to appease Nazi Germany by declaring a 'National Revolution' and replacing its traditional motto of 'Liberty, equality, fraternity' with 'Work, family, fatherland'; and what state of mind allowed anti-Jewish exhibitions to be held and French actors to dub into French such films as the well-known anti-Semitic production *Jew Süss* (1940) by Veit Harlan."[38]

---

38. *Le cinéma français, 1960-1985*, edited by Philippe de Comes and Michel Marmin in collaboration with Jean Arnoulx and Guy Braucourt, Editions Atlas, Paris, 1985.

Frédéric Rossif, *De Nuremberg à Nuremberg (From Nuremberg to Nuremberg)*

France (1989), television film, 180 min., black-and-white; language: French

Historical theme: reconstruction of the entire history of Nazism using archival material

Aesthetic theme: creative editing

The director

Frédéric Rossif was born in Montenegro in 1922 but left his country during the Second World War to move to France, where he took up a career in cinema and television. He became one of the pioneers of French television, specialising in documentaries about the arts (Picasso, Braque, Orson Welles, Jacques Brel), animals (*The Wilderness Party*, 1976; *L'Opéra sauvage*, 1977; *The Apocalypse of the Animals*, 1972) and war (*To Die in Madrid*, 1963; *The Witnesses*, 1961). He died in 1990.

The film

1. Cast

Commentary: Philippe Meyer

2. Background

The title emphasises the importance of Nuremberg, since the film begins with the Nazi party's mass rallies in this town from 1933 onwards, and especially the 1935 party congress, and finishes with the trial of certain Nazi leaders in 1946 for crimes against humanity. The Second World War began and ended in Nuremberg. Frédéric Rossif and Philippe Meyer provide a chronological account of the twelve years during which the Nazis ran Germany and decipher the reasons for Hitler's coming to power. They then precisely describe the concatenation of events that dragged the world into chaos, paying as much attention to the history of peoples and nations as to certain individual destinies. This documentary – made in 1987 for public television – was first broadcast two years later owing to censorship.

3. Analysis

In order that we may understand (in the words of journalist Philippe Meyer, who wrote the script) "why it was possible and how it was possible", Frédéric Rossif reconstructed the events of the Second World War and their multiple consequences. To this end he collected a considerable quantity of images and archive sequences (some of which had never been shown before), for which Philippe Meyer provided the commentary. The writer and the director, whose aim was above all to publicise the facts and analyse them rather than to create a moralising film, thus produced an invaluable teaching aid, even if some of the images are inevitably harrowing. They relate not only the battles on the different fronts (from Europe to the Pacific, taking in Africa on the way) but also daily life, the Occupation and the Resistance, using certain individual destinies to evoke the whole range of attitudes towards Nazism: from fanaticism to resistance, and from craven acceptance to brave indignation.

This remarkable summary is provided through a documentary film that is extremely rich. Frédéric Rossif's precise and pertinent editing of archival footage is excellently served by the sober commentary of Philippe Meyer, who has carefully selected Hitlerian texts to demonstrate that war, invasion and slaughter were planned and anticipated and that Hitler simply applied, without compunction, the ideas set out in *Mein Kampf*. The film's structure brings out the cold determination of the Nazi regime and its ideology. The music by Vangelis serves it to perfection.

4. Teaching suggestions

The film is divided into two parts, from which excerpts may be studied to explain particular events or analyse the form of the documentary.

a. Triumph and War (1933-1942)

Rossif gives a highly pedagogical explanation of Hitler's coming to power in 1933, the steps on the way to establishing a racist dictatorship, and the great Nazi rallies designed to fanaticise the Germans and prepare them for war. Walter Benjamin wrote that fascism was the "aestheticisation of politics". Hitler realised how he could turn film propaganda to his advantage. Reference is made to Hitler's coups, his tactical instinct, his ability to manipulate, and his double-dealing in promising not to invade Austria and Czechoslovakia and then disregarding his promises whilst turning the democracies' blindness and passivity to account. The war begins in 1939 with the invasion of Poland. The film then recounts the French campaign and the swift German victory. It highlights the way in which Hitler staged the signing of the armistice at Rethondes on 22 June 1940 (he arrived two hours late, ordered the railway coach in which the 1918 armistice was signed to be brought out, and took the place of the 1918 victors). The film next relates the Battle of Britain (Hitler's first setback against Churchill and British civilians) and shows how the war spread across the world (to the Pacific and Africa). He also demonstrates that Hitler's invasion of the USSR in 1941 was inevitable because of the German leader's deep-seated racism towards the Slavs.

b. Defeat and Judgment (1942-1945)

The second part, which is really a negative mirror image of the first, records the gradual crushing of Germany by the Allies: the capture of Italy, the Normandy landing and the liberation of France. The decisive confrontation was the Battle of Stalingrad, the Soviet victory which was the true turning point of the war. The Americans plunged into battle, paying the full price, as did the members of the French Resistance. Allied bombing of Germany razed the city of Dresden in one day with a toll of 250 000 deaths. The commentary shows how Hitler's intransigence and mistaken military tactics produced defeats, and it stresses his racism and determination to implement the "final solution". The last days of the Reich are a veritable funeral march orchestrated by a madman. The last pictures of Hitler show him celebrating his birthday in a ruined Berlin and unashamedly congratulating young recruits whom he is going to send to their deaths. The absolute madness of the man is encapsulated in these images. The last part of the film conscientiously explains the Nuremberg trial: the cold logic of the extermination camps and the genocide of the Jews, with the damning shots of the ghetto staged and filmed by the Nazis themselves. They draw the portrait of the defendants, who refuse to admit their responsibility and attempt to delay their inevitable conviction. We may cite an article by Agnès Bozon-Verduraz published in the French magazine *Télérama* when the film was first broadcast (15 November 1989):

'Covering' Nazism and the war on all fronts, including the Far East, in three hours is a feat in itself. Mastering the narrative balance is an achievement [...] Rossif, an extraordinary film editor, imparts to the archival material the rhythm of an animal in the throes of death. With its furious bursts of energy, its stumblings and its death rattles before the final collapse. Each scene forms a detailed part of this ghoulish chronology, with its pace, its powerful shots, its music, etc. The world is worse than a battlefield, a desolate planet where hard-pressed species go for each other's throats. It is as if the Nazis have communicated their lethal frenzy to the entire earth.

2. Documentaries with no historical documents

Claude Lanzmann, *Shoah*

France (1985), 540 min.; language: French

Historical theme: systematic destruction of European Jews

Moral theme: denunciation of a collective crime

Aesthetic themes: rejection of historical reconstruction, realism of eyewitness accounts, editing

The director

Born in Paris on 27 November 1925, Claude Lanzmann is a decorated member of the Resistance, an Officer of the Legion of Honour, a Commander of the National Order of Merit, and has an honorary PhD from the Hebrew University of Jerusalem. Since 1952 and his encounter with Jean-Paul Sartre and Simone de Beauvoir he has been a constant contributor to the journal *Les Temps modernes*, of which he is now editor. He has made *Why Israel?* (1973), *Shoah* (1985), *Tsahal* (1993), *A Visitor from the Living* (1997) and *Sobibor, October 14, 1943, 4 p.m.* (2002).

The film

1. Background

This is a film which takes place in the present and is shot in colour. Far from being "comforting fiction", it is meant to be "factual fiction" and presents brutality in a very different way from the sight of mass graves: through direct testimony about the gassing. There are various categories of witness: survivors still disturbed by what they lived through, former members of the SS denying all responsibility, Poles from Auschwitz and Birkenau still living in the houses from which Jews were expelled or in the immediate surroundings of the camps, and, lastly, survivors from the concentration camp death squads (*Sonderkommandos*) testifying to the atrocities that they witnessed. The circular structure is perfectly adapted to the compulsive questioning of a director looking for details of actual experience. As if the film were a work created not just by Lanzmann but also by his interviewees, the latter all carried out their duty of giving evidence to the bitter end, despite their suffering. Lastly, the historian Raul Hilberg, author of the monumental work *The Destruction of the European Jews*, explains the strategy of the Nazis, a logical continuation of Christian anti-Semitism. He subjects archival material and eyewitness accounts to scientific analysis and demonstrates that, to begin with, the Nazis were merely applying bureaucratic methods that had been tried and tested throughout Europe. They only became genuinely inventive when it was a matter of killing, for mass slaughter such as they were determined to perpetrate was unprecedented in history. Neither the Egyptian Pharaohs nor the

Babylonians – who were nevertheless anxious to get rid of the Jews – ever thought of the "final solution". The fourth-century missionaries said, "You may not live among us as Jews," and then secular rulers in the Middle Ages said, "You may not live among us." Finally, the Nazis decreed, "You may not live." Hence the unprecedented problem (how to kill as many people as possible at the same time) that Hitler's staff had to solve. He also analyses the economic exploitation of death: in the first place, transport at group rates, paid with money requisitioned from the victims themselves, as if they were going on package holidays. Then there was the technology of death, with first the invention of small gas chambers, then large ones and then lorries, initially using engine exhaust fumes before the notorious, more radical, Zyklon B. Thus the very idea of progress was hijacked for the sole end of organised crime.

2. Analysis

Prepared and shot over twelve years without a storyboard, this film was a fight against time and oblivion; it seeks to rediscover lost traces in disfigured places in order to counteract time and resurrect the event in all its horror. For, as Elie Wiesel declared when giving evidence at the Barbie trial: "To forget would be an absolute injustice in the same way that Auschwitz was the absolute crime. To forget would be the enemy's final triumph." Moreover, the Holocaust was such an indescribable crime that it immediately took on a legendary status. Lanzmann attempted to rescue it and restore the whole of its practical everyday reality by taking us to deceptively peaceful places still inhabited by people who witnessed or were involved in the killing. Encouraging them to speak amounts to rediscovering the living consciousness of past crimes buried in memory. Lanzmann's method is based on that of Marcel Ophüls but radicalises and sublimates it: asking key questions with a quiet sympathy designed to allay distrust, listening attentively until the witness becomes tangled up in his own answers, and exposing the weakness of his method of denial. The film-maker thus hounds the eyewitnesses into a corner, extracting unwittingly self-accusatory words from Poles and former Nazis and agonising memories from some of the survivors. Nobody meets anybody in *Shoah*, but the eyewitness accounts answer and follow on from each other thanks to inspired editing which reconstructs the hideous machine.

Furthermore, by compelling survivors to re-enact their past, despite their distress, Lanzmann makes them realise the importance of their testimony and the role they are playing in the great process of reconstruction and recollection and involves them in the making of his film. We may accuse him of having tormented them with his questions, but we know in reality that speaking is always a release and that silence has often been the lot of these survivors over many long years. Despite the horror they feel at revisiting these ghastly memories, they are therefore keen to testify in order to contribute to the writing of history with a capital "h". The scene in which the barber Abraham Bomba shows how he cut the hair of those going to the gas chambers will remain engraved in all our memories as a moment of almost intolerable emotion.

Trains still run through Auschwitz, Theresienstadt and Birkenau. Lanzmann takes us through these desolate landscapes to the mass grave which received what came out of the gas chambers, on the River Narew, that river which a Jewish child, saved by his melodious voice, descended every day singing German songs taught him by the SS. In these villages farmers live in houses formerly belonging to Jews and naïvely admit to being very pleased with their rise in the social hierarchy. Without showing any unbearable images, the film-maker reawakens in our imagination the hell of the stations and the freight trains that are now empty but were once crammed. Were there really rich bourgeois who arrived in Pullman cars, as the farmers claim? At all events, no Jewish person could suspect or imagine what was awaiting his people in these places where concealment was standard and a close watch was kept on language. The talk was of "disinfection", "work" and "information", and the prisoners were led naked to the deadly "shower". Administrative documents never refer to deaths or victims but speak of "transfers", "processing of units" and a "territorial solution". Raul Hilberg gives us a clear appreciation of the work necessary to relieve excessively obedient officials of all responsibility and to leave no written record of the slaughter. This has led some revisionists to deny the very existence of the camps. But Claude Lanzmann's images leave no room for doubt, and the eyewitness accounts that he has collected are unchallengeable. In particular, the interview with Jan Karski makes us wonder how the United States government could claim to know nothing about the Nazis' dealings.

3. Teaching suggestions

This film provides an incomparable history lesson and a perfect introduction to the methods of historical research. But it also raises the sensitive problem of the documentary, which, far from being a plain record of reality, always involves preparation, repetition and staging. Although the film's footage looks like video footage apparently filmed live, it should be pointed out that it is not. In *The Politics of Memory* Raul Hilberg recounts, for example, how Lanzmann borrowed a train from the Polish state, hired a retired train driver who had transported Jews to Treblinka and asked him to get behind the controls again. There is nothing wrong with this; students must simply be made aware that there are no films without a *mise en scène*, including documentaries. And Lanzmann was conscientious enough to harness his artistic talent to his subject and create a work of art (not an anonymous transcription such as Spielberg's, for example), with long-shot sequences showing the countryside and the natural beauty that has taken possession of the sites again and with shots from a car following a "Saurer" lorry (the make of the gas lorries).

The editing is the defining characteristic of this film, a film which simultaneously constitutes an irrefutable proof, an irreplaceable historical record and a tribute to all those dead men and women the memory of whom should render a recurrence of such horrors impossible. But above all it is a masterpiece of cinema, with a form that has been deliberately shaped to be best suited to its content and message, which accounts for its effectiveness.

Arnaud des Pallières, *Drancy Avenir*

France (1997), 84 min.; language: French

Historical theme: French collaboration in the systematic destruction of the Jews

Moral theme: denunciation of a collective crime

Aesthetic themes: rejection of historical reconstruction, eyewitness accounts, gap between past and present

The director

Arnaud des Pallières has built up a demanding oeuvre which challenges the very assumption on which documentaries are based. He is not interested in playing with the effect of belief stemming from a personal presence which guarantees the documentary maker's credibility; he wishes to reconstruct, after the event, a past in which he had no part and which does not concern him personally and to establish links between this past and the present which alone allows us to rediscover it. *Is Dead* (1999), a film about Gertrude Stein, and *Adieu* (2003) also play with this temporal discontinuity through rigorous editing and an original use of music to create tension.

The film

1. Cast

Aude Amiot: the student

Thierry Bosc: the history teacher

Anna-Lise Nathan: the singer

And the voices of Hanns Zischler, Jean-Paul Roussillon, Emma Soubrier and Adrien Faucheux

2. Background

This film, taking its name from a tram stop in the Parisian suburb of Bobigny and turning it into a symbol of hope, is not a documentary that makes use of eyewitnesses but a polyphonic work in which three narratives intersect: the memories of an elderly survivor; a young female student's investigation of the La Muette estate, a pre-war social housing complex where people still live; and the stories told by a captain on his boat, a metaphorical sequence which may allude to Dante, since it takes place on a wild river which seems to be that of Hell, the symbol of barbarity. The teacher/student device parallels that of the director's two previous films, *La mémoire d'un ange* and *Les choses rouges*. Using this didactic form, the film thus tries to give an impossible account of a history still quivering with everyday horror. Archival footage has been replaced by startling connections between the present-day setting and the evocation of memories associated with it. For the director says that "any work on the extermination is work not on the past but rather on the present".

3. Analysis

The voice-over seems to have reached the utmost limits of dejection when it begins this story of an obsession. The shot is innocuous: a window looking onto a park. Other sequences immediately follow on, taken from *The Merchant of Venice*, an unfinished film by Orson Welles in which Shylock appears as an emblem of exclusion. Then in German, over a shot of the French flag, another voice coldly declares that the silenced witnesses and destroyed evidence will render impossible an account of acts so dreadful that they are deliberately intended to challenge belief.

It is this challenge that Arnaud des Pallières takes up by attempting this impossible account in *Drancy Avenir*. He reconstructs the everyday horror of a history that is still very much alive, using a series of eyewitness accounts of one of the most odious episodes of France's recent past: the specific moment when, at the very gates of Paris, the French started vying with the Nazis in their imbecilic and criminal zeal to participate in the mass elimination of their Jewish compatriots. Writing this kind of history, which is barely beginning to emerge from the shadows of complicity, means drawing attention to de Gaulle's silence, the overzealousness of a too obedient administration, and the more or less deliberate blindness of the population.

There is no traumatising archival footage in this exemplary film. A walk through the present Drancy social housing estate establishes parallels between these perfectly linear buildings and the groups of huts in the camp. It is still the same inhuman concentration camp setting, but the bureaucrats filling in forms are simply social security staff, and the children playing in the snow have not been woken up at five in the morning and penned in like animals, ready to be deported. On the railway tracks, it is the same trains that pass each other, conjuring up the wagons into which people were crammed like cattle. Encouraging survivors to speak means stimulating memory and piecing together the jigsaw of individual recollections, the patchwork of eyewitness accounts. This is the director's strict and demanding objective. And if he has chosen modern images for this film, it is to argue the need to reflect time and again on the scars, still very fresh, of an experience so radical that it has become timeless.

As we can see, Arnaud des Pallières goes far beyond simple historical research. He shows with perfect restraint how an ordinary person can by slow degrees become a monster and inflict death at the stroke of a pen by drawing up lists and obeying his immediate superiors, and he demonstrates that this attempt to commit premeditated collective murder was partly successful because it overstepped the bounds of human reason. All those human beings crushed by their experience of this horror have tried to translate their anguish into words: a never-ending tunnel, a submerged submarine. They thus raise, in all simplicity, the great metaphysical questions: time, suffering, death, the origins and destiny of mankind. The film must be shown so that we may once again confront these fundamental issues, which are all too often pushed into the background by the immediate material concerns of daily life; *Drancy Avenir* must be shown so that we may forget nothing of what has poisoned our present and so that we may always be able to anticipate the future.

4. Teaching suggestions

Students should first be asked to define the limits of the three narrative stories and see how they intersect before trying to find which element of the Shoah matches each element of present-day life in Drancy (offices, children, tracks, trains, etc.), thus enabling them to understand the interplay of allusions and why the director chose to reject reconstruction in favour of a questioning of the present.

3. Protagonists and eyewitnesses

Emil Weiss, *Falkenau, vision de l'impossible (Falkenau, the Impossible)*

France (1988), 52 min., black-and-white/colour; languages: French and English

Historical theme: liberation of the camps by the Americans

Moral theme: denunciation of a collective crime

Aesthetic themes: rejection of historical reconstruction, realism of eyewitness accounts, film in a film

The director

Emil Weiss was born in 1947. An architect turned film-maker, he lives in Paris, where he has made numerous documentaries, including *Tell Me Sam* (1988-89), *Yeshayahou Leibowitz: Nul n'est prophète en son pays* (1989-91), *Israël Opus 40: Description d'une génération* (1992-93), *Quartier Lacan* (1994-96), *Léon Poliakov – Historien du racisme et de l'antisémitisme* (1994-96), *Destins – valeurs – transmissions – Rachel et Jacob Gordin* (1991-2002), *Mémoire d'Ernest* (2000-02), *La Mosaïque d'Alex Derczansky* (1996-2002), and *Secrets de silex: Dodi, l'homme qui fait parler la pierre* (2001-02). In 2002 he was awarded the Science, Art and Literature Prize of the Foundation for French Judaism.

The film

1. Background

In May 1945 the famous Big Red One – the First Infantry Division of the United States Army – fought its last European battle in the Sudeten Mountains in Czechoslovakia and liberated the Falkenau concentration camp. Samuel Fuller, an infantryman at the time, filmed this episode, and this unique documentary (16 mm, black-and-white, silent), hitherto unreleased, is included in *Falkenau, the Impossible*.

Following a brief introduction explaining the circumstances of the filming and the liberation of this typical camp, Samuel Fuller comments on the footage that he shot forty years earlier.

2. Analysis

"It's the only film where you see civilians in a camp doing what they do. It's the first and last time that happened during the war." This great film-maker, now departed, was aware of the uniqueness of what he had undertaken. The camera given to him by his father was the eye which he interposed between himself and the horror. He filmed on command but above all to etch in his memory the unique sight that met his eyes. In *Falkenau, the Impossible* he also ponders the problem of honesty in filming, the extent to which it is possible to represent the world of the concentration camp, and the need to pass on the memory to the younger generation.

3. Teaching suggestions

Through the double mediation of the director Sam Fuller, filming this tragic spectacle, and the director Emil Weiss, asking him about the circumstances of the filming, the film endeavours to understand the logic of the concentration camp system, whose only possible outcome was a crime against humanity. The liberation of the camps revealed its consequences. Archival footage discussed by the man who shot it, who later showed himself to be one of the great American film-makers, constitutes exceptional testimony. Emil Weiss has seized a unique opportunity to release archival material and make it available to the general public. The film-in-a-film device here takes on a heuristic role, since Fuller's footage is put into human, historical and cinematic perspective. Students should identify and comment on the relative scope of these different perspectives and their respective contributions to the film.

Rony Brauman and Eyal Sivan, *Un spécialiste, portrait d'un criminel moderne (The Specialist: Portrait of a Modern Criminal)*

Israel/France/Germany/Austria/Belgium (1999), 130 min.; language: French

Historical theme: Eichmann's trial in Jerusalem

Moral theme: how should a collective crime against humanity be punished?

Aesthetic themes: use of archival material, staging of history, role of eyewitnesses

The directors

Rony Brauman, a writer and teacher, was chairman of *Médecins sans Frontières* between 1982 and 1994. In Ethiopia in 1985 and Rwanda in 1994 he had an opportunity to observe the tragic consequences of what Hannah Arendt has called the politics of "the lesser evil". What he saw made him think that a passion to destroy was as much to blame as the mere passivity of ordinary people for the abominations perpetrated. Eyal Sivan, an Israeli dissident and documentary maker, was born in September 1964 in Haifa (Israel). He grew up in Jerusalem, left school before he had finished his education and devoted himself to photography. In 1982 during the Lebanese war he was declared unfit for military service by the Israeli army and became a fashion photographer before leaving Israel for France in 1985. He has worked on the use of memory and the fate of displaced Palestinians. Between 1987 and 1999 he made, amongst other films, *Aqabat Jaber: Passing Through*, *Israland* and *Jerusalem, Jerusalem*, as well as four short films on *Populations en danger*. The discovery in Jerusalem of hundreds of hours of archival footage of Eichmann's trial was the determining factor for him.

The film

1. Background

Rony Brauman and Eyal Sivan have borrowed from Hannah Arendt's book *Eichmann in Jerusalem: A Report on the Banality of Evil* to reconstruct the Eichmann trial and draw an intellectual portrait of its subject suggesting a person whose main quality was a concern for efficiency and a job well done. Important points are clarified. If Eichmann ended up in a key position in Nazi management, it was due to his strict method of working, which was much appreciated by his superiors, and his devotion to a cause which he said that he had never allowed himself to judge. From this point of view, the defendant's defence strategy in the Jerusalem trial becomes clearer: he admits having organised mass deportation of the Jews but disclaims any liability for the "final solution". He was merely processing the human material which it was his duty to transport, but the fate in store for these crowds of deportees was not, according to him, his responsibility.

In actual fact, like Raul Hilberg's book *The Destruction of the European Jews*, the film questions the system: a bureaucratic machine working in a highly compartmentalised manner. This division of labour lent itself perfectly to a watering-down of responsibilities. As both a military man and a bureaucrat, Eichmann had to obey unquestioningly. That was how he saw the matter. And that is how crime functions in a modern state. Scientists, technicians and clerks conscientiously carried out their work unhesitatingly, each at his post, without considering the immediate consequences of their obedience – or their zeal.

2. Analysis

"This normality was much more terrifying than all the atrocities put together," wrote Hannah Arendt.[39] Eichmann is a prime example of this, since the man was a model employee. Punctilious to the point of being finicky, he cleans his glasses and dusts the table holding the files, which he inspects with interest. His balding forehead, his glasses and his dark suit compound his serious appearance. He speaks what he himself calls "bureaucratic jargon": deadlines, schedules, quotas and orders. His main concerns: to respect the hierarchy and do his duty. Never taking any personal initiatives, he did no more than scrupulously obey the orders that he received.

Language proved to be the ideal instrument for this routine work. A whole vocabulary was created in order to disembody the field in which these officials worked: "mustering", "evacuation", "transfer", "special treatment" and "final solution". In the same way that officials dissociated themselves from their duties, words were drained of meaning in order that they might appear in apparently innocuous documents. In one scene in the film, Eichmann says that he was shocked when, at the Wannsee Conference between glasses of brandy, he heard talk of methods of killing in terms too blunt for his liking. Just for once, his superiors had shown their true faces, and the language had caused his administrative veneer to crack.

The film-makers have done substantial work on the archival material. The five hundred hours of footage shot during the trial were in large part unusable. The Spielberg Archive had extracted seventy hours from it, the only footage deemed original and useable. Brauman and Sivan established a new stock from the original archival material by digitally remastering it. They have selected moments from the trial reflecting various historical episodes concerning which the defendant's account was corroborated by those of the witnesses. Little by little the character of the "specialist", his field of activity and his expert knowledge thus became apparent. Certain themes emerge from the editing of sequences: the administration's hierarchical structure, the limits of the defendant's powers, the cumbersome process of deportation, and the general functions and specific role of the "*Judenräte*" (Jewish councils), the select bodies through which the Nazis

---

39. *Eichmann à Jérusalem. Rapport sur la banalité du mal*, Gallimard, 1963, p. 444.

delegated operations to the Jewish authorities themselves. Thirteen moments from the trial have thus been singled out and put together in chronological order to demonstrate that fundamental aspect of the Nazi system: the organisation of a state crime.

3. Teaching suggestions

The problem of using archival material is worth addressing and discussing with students. The original footage has been completely remodelled. Digital lighting has given it depth, camera movements have given a new dynamism to long shots put together from a number of partial shots, and the resulting video was transferred onto 35 mm film using a new IT technique. The original soundtrack has been replaced by recordings of the main players in the trial made by the Kol Israel radio station and has been entirely resynchronised, while sound effects have been added to recreate the sounds of the courtroom. The very possibility of such reshaping of visual and sound archives may be considered worrying. If raw material can be transformed in this way using modern technology, is this not an open invitation to every kind of manipulation? Furthermore, this work was undertaken to illustrate Hannah Arendt's argument; it was therefore guided by an ideological position which determined its choice of footage. However much we may feel that Rony Brauman and Eyal Sivan were working in a good cause and that cinema would not exist without special effects, we here come up against an important point of professional ethics which must be discussed. Having said this, we cannot but welcome an undertaking which, by means of intelligent restoration, shows new generations the courtroom drama of Eichmann's trial and enables them to understand the process of dissociation and abstraction through which an ordinary man was able to commit monstrous acts and, like Pontius Pilate, to whom he compares himself, wash his hands of them. The normality of the murderer, more terrifying than everything, as noticed by Hannah Arendt, is the lesson of the film. It shows the starkest form of "barbarity with a human face" (after the title of Bernard-Henri Lévy's book, 1977). The "patriotic bureaucracy" dear to the psychoanalyst Pierre Legendre[40] came up with an "inoffensive" barbarity and perpetrated that modern form of crime, which is administrative crime implicating an entire people.

---

40. *Jouir du pouvoir. Traité de la bureaucratie patriote*, Editions de minuit, 1976.

Claude Lanzmann, *Sobibor, 14 octobre 1943, 16 heures (Sobibor, 14 October 1943, 4 p.m.)*

France (2002), 90 min., colour; language: French

Historical theme: the Sobibor camp and the escape of Yehuda Lerner

Moral theme: collective crime and the reappropriation of violence by the Jews

Aesthetic themes: rejection of historical reconstruction, realism of eyewitness accounts, from history to legend

The director

Born in Paris on 27 November 1925, Claude Lanzmann is a decorated member of the Resistance, an Officer of the Legion of Honour, a Commander of the National Order of Merit, and has an honorary PhD from the Hebrew University of Jerusalem. Since 1952 and his encounter with Jean-Paul Sartre and Simone de Beauvoir he has been a constant contributor to the journal *Les Temps modernes*, of which he is now editor. He has made *Why Israel?* (1973), *Shoah* (1985), *Tsahal* (1993), *A Visitor from the Living* (1997) and *Sobibor* (2002).

The film

1. Cast

Yehuda Lerner

2. Background

The Sobibor camp occupies a central position in *Shoah*, but no Jewish protagonists in the revolt were asked to provide eyewitness accounts in that film because Lanzmann felt that Sobibor, being an example of what he has called "the reappropriation of power and violence by the Jews", deserved a film of its own, whose emblematic hero would be Yehuda Lerner. This indomitable man symbolises individual bravery in these camps where Jews were supposed to have allowed themselves to be killed unsuspectingly and unresistingly. It is fair to say that the Jews were not prepared to use violence, having neither the temperament nor an acquaintance with weapons (who does in peacetime?). And it took a Jewish officer of the Red Army, Alexander Pechersky, conversant with the military, to organise the Sobibor uprising. Lanzmann thus follows Lerner's course through the eight camps from which he successively escaped, before allowing him to recount the extraordinary adventure of the Sobibor uprising. The film is in two parts: Lerner's personal odyssey, and the hatching of the plot. It alternates lateral tracking shots, filmed from trains crossing Poland in all directions, with static shots, from various distances, which follow Lerner's account. From escape to active imprisonment, Lerner gives the world an amazing lesson in courage and tenacity. His surprisingly young face puts us in mind of the sixteen-year-old boy brutally separated from his parents and faced with the worst of ordeals. The youthful elation that he re-experiences upon recalling the moment when he killed a Nazi officer with an axe is belied by an almost absent-minded smile which emphasises the gulf between his personality and a murderer's and the time that has elapsed between that fateful day and the present. The measured tone which he uses to reply to Lanzmann's questions is somewhat dramatised by his interpreter, Francine Kaufmann, who tends to emphasise the extraordinary nature of his feats. Such is the *mise en scène* of this exemplary film, where speech echoes back from each of the three characters to the two others to bring out the heroism of one man.

3. Analysis

With his film *Shoah*, Claude Lanzmann invented a cinematic genre – the documentary with no archival material, consisting of present-day eyewitness accounts of crucial events – and thus rendered irredeemably obsolete the editing of more or less authentic archival footage that had been a feature of previous films about the extermination of the Jews. This method, which has now become the norm, is used in *Sobibor*. "We had", says Lerner, as if to vindicate himself, "to react to such unbelievable barbarity." And we realise that the great weakness of the victims of Nazism was that they were unable to imagine what awaited them. Was it conceivable for the passengers in the Sobibor trains that they were going to be burned, as they had been informed by a Polish pointsman? And why try to escape if they did not believe this? How is it possible to enter the mindset of barbarism? Or imagine the systematic destruction of six million individuals? These are some of the central questions raised by the film. One detail out of thousands: the Germans claimed that the Jews died "honking like geese". It defies belief that they bolstered this base comparison by releasing into nearby fields real gaggles of geese whose noise was to cover the cries of people being put to death. This sequence in the film is a good illustration of the way in which Lanzmann works, emphasising harshest reality with unbearably poetic metaphorical images. The merit of those who resisted at Sobibor was to appropriate the mindset of their killers and rely on German punctuality in planning individual and simultaneous attacks (at 4 p.m. precisely) in various parts of the camp. What a lesson in strategy!

4. Teaching suggestions

Show how this brief film (approximately one and a half hours long), which centres on an almost mythical hero – an undernourished David striking an all-powerful Goliath with all his feeble strength – has left the realm of history to enter that of legend. Evoking the world of mythology and the cinema of Chaplin, Hitchcock and Clint Eastwood with its symbolism, this film will appeal to our students – so responsive to individual heroism – and make history come alive for them. And it will be a long time before they forget the example set by this boy – almost a child – who boldly and irreproachably confronts the very symbol of Nazi barbarism. But you should point out to them that the legend may also be regarded as too heroic to be representative and that a wide range of forms of resistance, doubtless less spectacular, had existed well before the Sobibor uprising.

B. Other views

Katherine Smalley, *So Many Miracles*

Canada (1986), 48 min.; language: English

Historical theme: return to the sites of the Shoah

Aesthetic theme: reporting as a means of giving a voice to people who have had remarkable experiences

The director

Katherine Smalley was born in Ontario in 1946. After studying politics and philosophy at Montreal, Toronto and Amsterdam she worked in the financial sector and communications whilst writing, making films and lecturing. Katherine Smalley's mastery of reporting has brought her a number of awards, including the Gabriel award for best documentary feature in the United States.

The film

1. Cast

The director herself, Saul Rubinek, his parents and the Polish woman, Zofia Banya

2. Background

Forty years later, the Rubineks, a Jewish family of Polish origin, return to the house where a Polish peasant woman concealed them for over three years at the risk of her life.

3. Analysis

The film-maker Katherine Smalley read Saul Rubinek's book about the extraordinary story of his parents, who were concealed from November 1942 to February 1945 by a Polish peasant woman and her family in a small hiding place on their farm. She decided to make a film of it. The story of this young couple, married at 21, is indeed enough to touch anyone. Young Frania belonged to the *shtetl* of Pinczow and led the simple life of her mother and grandmother before her. Israel lived in Lodz and was much more broad-minded; he had broken with his

Hassidic traditions and become committed to Zionism. He also acted in Yiddish plays and danced the tango. Frania needed nothing more to fall in love with him at sixteen when he came visiting his grandparents in the *shtetl*. In 1940, before the Lodz ghetto was created and Jews were prohibited from leaving it, Israel took off his Star of David and travelled 250 kilometres to join his grandparents and Frania. One year later he and Frania were married and opened a grocery for the local farmers. But Israel, worried by the rumours about the Germans' intention of exterminating the Jews, dug a bunker to hide his family, which they used for the Jewish New Year in autumn 1942 when the first deportations reached the village of Pinczow. Frania was eight months pregnant. When all the family left for Lublin, she tried to persuade her husband to leave without her, but he refused.

At this juncture, they heard of a peasant woman who was looking for them. They had allowed her credit, which was not done at the time, and she wanted to thank them by saving their lives. They went to see her, hidden in a hay wagon, and were sheltered in her humble cottage together with her husband Ludwig and her seven-year-old son Maniek. They stayed there for over two years. Frania lost her child in labour. Later her brother and sister, who had by pure chance rented a flat in Warsaw from Ludwig's sister, thus learnt where she was hidden and sent her money to join them as soon as possible.

4. Teaching suggestions

So Many Miracles is not just a film about the Rubineks' exceptional good luck; it is a film about gratitude. For forty years the Rubineks kept in touch with Zofia and her family through letters, regularly sending them clothes and money. Ludwig is now dead, and Maniek is over sixty. He was fifty when, in August 1986, Israel and Frania returned to Pinczow to see Zofia. Their son Saul went with them, which was for him an extraordinarily moving experience. He has turned it into a book, and Katherine Smalley has turned it into a film. The film is particularly touching, showing courageous Poles ready to risk their lives to save their Jewish friends – and allowing us to experience the deeply moving moment of their reunion.

Some work could be done on Jewish life in Poland before the Shoah – the *shtetl*, Orthodox Jews and the Hassidim – so as to give students an idea of the diversity of the Jewish world in Poland, which was not "a community" but rather a fairly disparate group of people practising the same religion in different ways.

Dan Weissman, *Terezin Diary*

United States (1989), 88 min.; language: English

Historical themes: story of the children in the Theresienstadt camp, Nazi window-dressing of the horror

Aesthetic themes: re-establishing a stubbornly denied truth through words and images, creative editing of disparate elements

The director

Dan Weissman's film about Judaic treasures from Czechoslovakia, *The Precious Legacy*, has won a number of awards. Zuzana Justman, the writer and executive producer of *Terezin Diary*, was the driving force behind the latter film. Herself a Terezin survivor, she developed the idea of the film and conducted most of the interviews.

The film

1. Cast

Zuzana Justman, Dan Weissman, James E. Young and the voice of Eli Wallach as narrator

2. Background

In 1941 the Nazis turned Theresienstadt, an old fortress town near Prague, into a concentration camp. Their intention, well attested by the documents in our possession, was to create a model camp to feature in their propaganda. In reality, Terezin was a stop on the way to the camps in the East, and the 140 000 prisoners who passed through it, including 15 000 children, lived in huts crammed to bursting point, racked by hunger and disease and faced with the constant threat of deportation to Auschwitz. At least 33 000 people died in Terezin. This film tells their story and that of their children, in particular Helga Kinsky, who arrived at Terezin at the age of twelve with her father. Helga Kinsky kept a very careful diary of her life in the camp. This diary begins on 17 January 1943, the day on which she was dragged from her home in a small town in Moravia and put on a train for Terezin, and ends on 23 October 1944 when she was sent to Auschwitz without her father.

3. Analysis

In 1986 some of the Terezin children, now aged over 50, met in Prague: the film begins with this reunion. It mixes together survivors' memories, passages from Helga's diary and the diary of her father, works of art, children's drawings, archival material and footage from a German propaganda film made about the camp. It follows Helga and the other survivors in their journey from the Terezin "family camp" to Auschwitz. It ends with Helga's return to Terezin, a meeting with her father after the war, and images of Helga today with her daughter and granddaughter.

With nine other camp survivors, Helga describes the strange paradox of this model ghetto, in which the children could see a pianist on the roof one day and a death transport the next, for Terezin was not a place of permanent horror. The SS did their utmost to give it the appearance of a normal town, going so far as to open it to Red Cross inspectors for a day. But prior to the inspection the SS had deported 7 500 people to Auschwitz so that the camp would look less crowded, and they had hastily decorated and embellished it. They took the inspectors on a guided tour of a brand new building, specially constructed for the occasion, with a hall where Verdi's *Requiem* was performed in concert.

The well-known artists – writers, actors, musicians – who came to Terezin from all over central Europe actually worked and gave performances, and the concentration of cultural activity there was amazing. The Nazis also referred to Terezin as the "ghetto of the elders". They attracted elderly German Jews who paid fortunes to have so-called luxury apartments. The lives of the children at Terezin were undoubtedly made easier by the Jewish Council, but its power was limited. The children were protected, encouraged to draw and publish their own magazines, and put on the famous opera *Brundibar*. However, only one in ten of these children survived their stay in Terezin.

4. Teaching suggestions

In another film, *Voices of the Children*, Zuzana Justman uses personal diaries and drawings kept by men and women who were interned in the Terezin camp. Now adults, they thus relive their tortured childhood in this camp in which a true "concentration of culture" was created. Their horrifying eyewitness accounts absolutely give the lie to the notorious Nazi propaganda films which implied that the camp was a little paradise. After the success of the Red Cross visit, the Germans used Terezin for their propaganda in a film showing "Hitler's beneficence to the Jews". A very rare clip from this film is shown as damning evidence in *Terezin Diary*. It is important to stress the ironic use made of it. Through parallel editing the director contrasts the children's games filmed by the Nazis with accounts of the actual living conditions in the camp so as to produce a very different truth. The gap between propaganda and reality is thus exposed.

Marian Marzynski, *Shtetl: A Journey Home*

United States (1996), 175 min.; language: Polish, English subtitles

Historical theme: social consequences of the Shoah

Aesthetic themes: rejection of historical reconstruction, the present challenged by the past

The director

A Polish Jew who survived the Shoah, Marian Marzynski has made a number of documentaries about his experience of forced emigration, from *Return to Poland* (1981) and *Jewish Mother* (1982) to *God Bless America and Poland Too* (1990), *Our Man in Russia* (1993) and *Skin Deep* (1995). *Shtetl* was awarded the Grand Prix at the Cinéma du Réel Festival in Paris in 1995.

The film

1. Cast

The director himself, his friend Nathan, and Zbyszek Romaniuk

2. Background

First, Marian Marzynski accompanies his friend Nathan on the trail of his family from Bransk, a small town in Poland. There they meet Zbyszek Romaniuk, a young Polish man who is a local scholar and with whom the director has been exchanging letters for some time. All three examine sites and various witnesses to try to rediscover the now obliterated marks of the Jewish past in Bransk and understand the erstwhile living conditions in the *shtetl*. But the *shtetl* disappeared without trace when 2 500 Jews were deported to Treblinka.

In the second part of the film, Zbyszek goes to the United States to meet Jewish families originally from Bransk who manage to recall some memories.

The third part of the film shows Zbyszek going to pursue his investigations in Israel. But here he is faced with young students who reproach him with the anti-Semitism of his fellow citizens and the Polish in general.

Finally, back in Bransk, he is criticised and threatened because of his interest in Jewish history, deemed suspect and excessive. These criticisms do not prevent him from subsequently becoming deputy mayor of his small town, but he is obliged to forgo his interest in this aspect of his past.

3. Analysis

In this investigation, exemplary in its rigour and conducted patiently over the long term, we again find the interview technique developed by Claude Lanzmann in *Shoah* – a technique that reaches the same conclusions, moreover. It succeeds in making clear the socio-historical sources of Polish anti-Semitism: that basic envy felt by the poor peasants towards the affluent bourgeois who controlled the village economy. Appropriating their property seemed to these peasants to be redress of a profound injustice.

4. Teaching suggestions

It would be appropriate to compare this film with the sequence shot by Lanzmann in the Polish village near Auschwitz and to show the precise workings of the interviewing technique that consists in making people say exactly what is expected of them, which they are unable to hide – no doubt because they do not even feel themselves to be guilty.

Ruth Beckermann, *Jenseits des Krieges (East of War)*

Austria (1996), 117 min., colour; language: German

Historical theme: present-day eyewitness accounts by protagonists and witnesses of the Shoah in Austria

Aesthetic theme: the present marked by the past

The director

Born in Vienna into a Jewish family from Bukovina, Ruth Beckermann, a writer and film-maker, has devoted her work to investigating the ghosts of her native town in order to rescue it from collective amnesia at last. She has published *Die Mazzelsinsel* (1984), *Unzugehörig* (1989) and *Ohne Untertitel (Without Subtitles: Fragments of a History of Austrian Cinema*, 1996). She has also made a film trilogy: *Return to Vienna* (1984), *The Paper Bridge* (1987) and *Toward Jerusalem* (1990).

The film

1. Cast

The director herself, her cameraman, and former Wehrmacht soldiers

2. Background

The film takes as its subject an exhibition of photographs held in Vienna about Wehrmacht crimes between 1941 and 1944, entitled "War of Extermination" (*Vernichtungskrieg*). This exhibition was put together by the Hamburg Institute for Social Research and was shown in German and Austrian cities before reaching Vienna, where it was accommodated in the converted premises of the old central dairy in 1995.

3. Analysis

The black-and-white photographs were exhibited in an antiseptic setting – white-tiled rooms and harsh neon lighting. The director and her cameraman have filmed interviews with visitors, in which former soldiers recollect their past. In these private sessions they talk about themselves and their experiences on the Eastern Front, "east of the war", and beyond the bounds of "normal" warfare. Were the visitors interviewed – perfectly ordinary people – perpetrators, members of the Resistance, or passive witnesses of the slaughter? Very few of them admit to having killed voluntarily. But they all acknowledge having believed in an "ideology" and having supported "preventive action against Bolshevism". "We experienced this war differently from what is shown here", they say. An excellent lesson in relativism ... or deliberate blindness. Their versions of what happened vary considerably, demonstrating how selective, whether in good or bad faith, perception of these events can be, whatever the circumstances. Some evince shame, embarrassment and despondency, others opportunism and undiminished fanaticism. Their accounts are of executions of Soviet prisoners of war, murder of Jews and the rape of women. These "thousand memories" of former soldiers confronted with their past together weave a collective history made topical again by Haider's rise to power: a past that refuses to go away.

4. Teaching suggestions

Emphasis should be laid on the problem of truth and falsehood, or rather the repression of a heinous past in which these men played an active part or to which they were witnesses. Some are speaking for the first time, releasing themselves from what they have seen and the suffocating silence in which they had taken refuge. Others persist in denial. These are survival strategies when forgetting is the only option.

A historical clarification: in 1938 the Viennese acclaimed Hitler on the Heldenplatz, yet the historiographic myth in Austria is of an invasion by the Nazis in 1938, as clearly stated in the 1955 State Treaty which restored the country's sovereignty. Ruth Beckermann's film challenges another myth, that of the "decent" Wehrmacht. Two myths for such a small country is a lot. The Austrians "just did their duty", to use Kurt Waldheim's phrase. Their policy of silence coupled with their traditional lightheartedness has, for decades, suggested a misleading innocence. But the violent reactions aroused by the exhibition and the extremely high suicide rate in Austria shows the truth to be rather different. Such silences, which also exist in other countries, must be broken if the population is to hold up its head.

Tsipi Reibenbach, *Shalosh Ahayot (Three Sisters)*

Israel (1997), 68 min., colour; language: Hebrew, English subtitles

Historical theme: aftermath of the camps, their far-reaching effects on inmates' lives

Moral theme: denunciation of a collective crime

Aesthetic theme: the interview as an attempt to comprehend the incomprehensible

The director

Tsipi Reibenbach studied physics and mathematics at Tel Aviv University before obtaining a degree in film, television and animation there. She has been a past master in the making of documentaries ever since her first full-length film *Widow Plus* (1981), a portrait of five young women widowed by the Yom Kippur war. Filmed between 1988 and 1993, *Choice and Destiny*, which won a number of awards, is a portrait of her parents. Her following film, *Three Sisters*, also received multiple awards. Between 2000 and 2003 she made *A City with No Pity*.

The film

1. Cast

The director's mother and aunts

2. Background

Fruma, Ester and Karola are three septuagenarian sisters living in Tel Aviv in 1996. Survivors from the camps, they experience their old age with a kind of amazement as a last chance. Tsipi Reibenbach encourages her mother and aunts to talk in order to understand their lives and probe their wounds. Memory is their main resource.

3. Analysis

Ester was the prettiest of the three sisters, or at any rate the most courted. She even thinks that her brother-in-law was in love with her. Nowadays she visits her husband daily in a rest home but tries to make the most of life by doing all the things that she likes: going to the beach, watching television series and playing cards. Her husband died while the film was being made, leaving a great gap in her life. Karola, who has lost interest in life, has found company in an old people's home but is still depressed and tries to kill herself. Fruma, the director's mother, tirelessly writes her memoirs on the kitchen table and accompanies her husband to his numerous check-ups. These three sisters, who spend hours talking to each other on the telephone, are all faced with the same haunting question: how is it possible to accept being old so soon when you have lost your youth in a concentration camp?

Tsipi Reibenbach follows these three survivors bound together by an oppressive past: at the beach, in hospital, at home. Patiently she questions them. Ester's humour, Fruma's stubbornness and Karola's sadness are their defence mechanisms. They are readier to recount their love affairs than their ordeals. But the burden sometimes weighs so heavily that they lay it down in front of the camera. It is a strength of cinema that it manages to capture these scarcely perceptible cracks: a voice that falters, a look that becomes absent, a gesture indicative of long-controlled grief. The affection of the niece and daughter is apparent in every shot and above all the infinite respect in which she holds these wounded women who brought her up. Although she is readier to film their smiles than their tears, she constantly expresses her compassion for and fascination with the extreme horror that they have experienced, which defies word and image.

4. Teaching suggestions

Three Sisters is interesting for the use it makes of what is off-screen. We know that the film structure is, above all, a mask and is important less for what it reveals than for what it conceals; this film takes pleasure in harmless scenes of peaceful daily life only the better to evoke, in the negative, the long wasted years. Discretion here takes the place of emphasis. Silence is as important as speech. An attempt should be made to reconstruct orally and in writing everything that it does not show.

PART TWO
AMERICAN FICTION FILMS

1. Examples of realism

Marvin J. Chomsky, *Holocaust*

United States (1978), television mini-series, 475 min., colour; language: English

Historical theme: from the rise of Nazism to the concentration camps, the whole history of Nazism through the life of a German family

Aesthetic themes: historical reconstruction and overstatement

The director

Born in 1929, the American director Marvin Chomsky has a considerable body of work to his name as director, producer and set designer. He has made history programmes and dramas such as *Catherine the Great* (1995) and *The Strauss Dynasty* (1991), but his most famous is undoubtedly *Holocaust*.

The film

1. Cast

Fritz Weaver: Dr Josef Weiss

James Woods: Karl Weiss

Joseph Bottoms: Rudi Weiss

Sam Wanamaker: Moses Weiss

Blanche Baker: Anna Weiss

Meryl Streep: Inga Helms Weiss

Rosemary Harris: Berta Palitz Weiss

Michael Moriarty: Erik Dorf

Deborah Norton: Marta Dorf

Ian Holm: Heinrich Himmler

Tom Bell: Adolph Eichmann

2. Background

The Weiss family, a typical family of educated middle-class Jews resident in Berlin, suffer the repercussions of the historical events through which they are living: the rise of Nazism, deportation to Auschwitz and Theresienstadt, and departure for

Palestine. There are thus two parallel stories in the film: the "final solution" as suffered by the Weiss family, and the successive stages in the planning of the elimination of the European Jews.

3. Analysis

The film consists of four parts:

Part 1: *The Gathering Darkness* (145 min.)

Part 2: *The Road to Babi Yar* (105 min.)

Part 3: *The Final Solution* (100 min.)

Part 4: *The Saving Remnant* (120 min.)

Part 1

Berlin, 1935: Karl Weiss, the artist son of prosperous Jewish doctor Josef Weiss, marries Inga Helms, a Catholic girl. At the same time Marta, wife of lawyer Erik Dorf, whose family are Dr Weiss's patients, persuades her husband to join the SS. Their stories run parallel.

Part 2

Warsaw, 1941: deported to Poland, Josef Weiss and his wife are involved in organising the Warsaw Ghetto in order to combat despair and their atrocious living conditions. Soon the first signs of an active resistance appear. In Buchenwald, Karl is arrested and tortured following a brawl.

Part 3

1942: German troops are advancing to the East. As they move forward, mobile SS units round up and massacre Jews. The Jewish partisan brigade led by "Uncle Sasha" engages in fierce combat.

Part 4

In Poland, in Warsaw, Josef and Berta Weiss are ordered onto the next train for what is called a "family camp". During this time, the Resistance fighters, who have managed to hide and survive, join forces and rise up in the Warsaw Ghetto.

As Annette Insdorf points out (in *Indelible Shadows*), the merit of this television series is to have drawn the general public's attention to Nazi atrocities previously studied only by historians. But can one make historical fiction out of such a subject? Furthermore, this "docudrama" introduces a certain element of confusion by deliberately blurring the boundary between fiction and reality and between history in general and one family's individual story, since Chomsky worked on the assumption that it would be easier for viewers to identify with a family like their own and thus to understand the historical problems scaled down to this family context.

Television has undoubtedly become our main window on the world, moulding our collective consciousness and standardising the substratum of our experience. *Holocaust* marks the arrival of the Shoah with a Jewish perspective in the world of popular entertainment. This historical thriller had a considerable impact in the United States, making most people aware of what had happened, and in Germany, where the word "holocaust" began simultaneously to denote the genocide, the film and the audience reaction. The film's popularising effect is indisputable and a perfect example of how Hollywood portrays political issues, applying a hackneyed dramatic form to new material so as to respect marketing requirements that impose certain conventions such as constant recourse to pathos or terror. It is the exact opposite of Resnais's rule, namely, the more emotional the material, the less emotional the treatment.

4. Teaching suggestions

You should therefore show how there is an escalation of pathos and a recourse to manipulative sentimentalism which can only diminish the film's emotional force. Thus the ending clearly ministers to the American sensibility: there is only one survivor from the Weiss family, and he leaves for Palestine. Should we see this as an echo of Abraham Hershel's philosophy that the affirmation of life after destruction baffles despair? The protests of Elie Wiesel, according to whom the Shoah transcends history and representation, have not weakened the impact of this film, which has produced a salutary awareness despite the inevitable trivialisation accompanying it. Overstatement is probably more effective in getting over a strong message to a mass audience.

Steven Spielberg, *Schindler's List*

United States (1994), historical fiction, 195 min.; language: English

Historical theme: life of a German who fights Nazism and saves Jews

Moral themes: a human and political choice under an iniquitous regime, end and means

Aesthetic themes: historical reconstruction, realism

The director

Born in Cincinnati, Ohio, in 1947, Steven Spielberg quickly started shooting his first short films with his father's Super-8 camera. By the age of 13 he was already writing his own scripts, drawing his own very detailed storyboards and even composing the music for his films. At 14 he made his first "real" short film, *Escape to Nowhere*, which recreated Field Marshal Rommel's campaigns. He became fascinated by science fiction and in 1964 shot *Firelight*, a film with a budget of 500 dollars. But 1964 was also the year in which his parents divorced, a date of cardinal importance which was to mark all his future work, where stories of broken families make a regular appearance. Caught up in the family upheaval, he moved to California and was turned down by a film school; he consequently enrolled at California State University to study English. But his four years at university allowed him above all to build up his cinema knowledge. During this period he discovered European cinema, made various experimental films and watched a great many. In 1968 he made his first 35 mm short film called *Amblin'* with the help of Allen Daviau, future director of photography for *E.T.*, *The Colour Purple* and *Empire of the Sun*. *Duel*, Spielberg's first television film, was a triumphant success in Europe. David Brown and Richard D. Zanuck offered this young talent the chance to shoot his first full-length film, *Sugarland Express*. The following year, with the release of *Jaws*, Spielberg joined the top ranks of young American film-makers. The consecration was to come two years later with *Close Encounters of the Third Kind*. With his friend George Lucas, Spielberg was now becoming ambitious. Between them they developed the idea for the film *Raiders of the Lost Ark*. The project materialised in 1981, with what success we well know. Strengthened by his reputation, Steven Spielberg made *E.T.*, the film that he felt must logically follow from *Close Encounters of the Third Kind*. Released in 1982, *E.T.* held the United States box-office record for eleven years – a record shattered by *Jurassic Park*. The money generated by the adventures of the archaeologist played by Harrison Ford enabled Spielberg to change register completely and shoot *The Colour Purple*, a film which received eleven Oscar nominations. *Empire of the Sun* and *Schindler's List* were also nominated for Oscars.

Spielberg has two very engaging character traits: he has remained a child, and for this child the cinema is the most wonderful toy possible. He thus communicates his child's-eye view to the audience; in all his films we notice the presence of children through whose eyes we see the action. In addition, he is a generous and committed man who is anxious that his work should speak in favour of the causes in which he believes and to which he attaches enormous importance: protection of nature, awareness of the extermination of the Jews during the war, and black slavery. The hundreds of hours of eyewitness accounts that he has had recorded with survivors of the Shoah constitute irreplaceable evidence that will make revisionism impossible.

The film

1. Cast

Liam Neeson: Oskar Schindler

Ben Kingsley: Itzhak Stern

Ralph Fiennes: Amon Goeth

Caroline Goodall: Emilie Schindler

2. Background

The film relates the story of Oskar Schindler, that extraordinary German businessman who, when the Jews were being expelled, developed a plan to resist the Nazi system. Becoming friendly with the most powerful men of the Reich, finding Jewish investors in an occupied population in utter disarray, restarting a kitchenware factory and obtaining lucrative military orders from the Armaments Inspectorate were the successive stages of his programme up to early 1940. But the most original aspect of this venture was the systematic recruitment, from then on, of Jewish workers, considered less expensive, in fact unpaid, since Schindler paid a fee for each of them to SS Headquarters in Krakow.

3. Analysis

A low-angle shot provides a close-up of a solitary figure in the middle of a nightclub. Dressed in a light-coloured suit, smiling and relaxed, he tells the waiter that he is standing a round for the Nazi officers seated across the room. They thank him, come to join him and spend a very lively and well-oiled evening in his company. This is Krakow in 1939. The opening sequence of Spielberg's film *Schindler's List*, based on Thomas Keneally's novel, indicates the first part of Schindler's plan. The film then analyses the amazing personality of this German whose charm made him an unrepentant womaniser, one of the liveliest revellers in this Nazi-occupied society and at the same time a human being able to use this charm to maximise his profit from the war industry, accumulate a fabulous fortune and use this fortune to save over a thousand Jews. Schindler is magnificently played by Liam Neeson. Claude Lanzmann has criticised Spielberg for having chosen a "good" German for his hero and given him undeniable glamour. This controversy filled the newspapers at the time. Schindler's power behind the throne, Itzhak Stern, is played by the excellent Ben Kingsley and is Schindler's mirror image. The accountant and right-hand man who enabled Schindler to become one of the wealthiest businessmen of the Reich works behind the scenes recruiting Jews who are more or less skilled and balancing the books of this enormous enterprise.

The film raises a real problem of cinema ethics. We may ask whether the director of *Jurassic Park* was the best man to portray such a subject. Can one apply the same tricks of the trade to dinosaurs and to the martyrdom of the Jews in Poland? Spielberg foresaw these reservations. He has endeavoured – as far as possible – to work like a reporter, capturing reality in almost documentary fashion in order to have an authentic approach to the historical context. His sets? The city of Krakow itself, preserved from the ravages of war, Schindler's actual factory and his apartment, which have remained unchanged, as well as a faithful reconstruction of the Plaszow forced labour camp based on the plans of the original camp. The director chose to film in black-and-white to parallel the archival material of the time and worked painstakingly on the photography with his cinematographer Janusz Kaminski.

4. Teaching suggestions

It might be shown that Spielberg is subject to Hollywood marketing requirements all the same. He cannot avoid emphasising the pathos of the story, especially in the final scenes. He even uses fantastical special effects for documentary purposes when Schindler, out riding with his mistress, sees from a hilltop the carnage being perpetrated across the ghetto and the famous little girl in red whom he follows until she disappears inside a house. For children are omnipresent here as in all his films. In other respects, the director highlights the horrible nature of nudity in the camps in contrast with the eroticism of the love scenes. But what he demonstrates perfectly, above all, and what can consequently be studied in class is the bureaucratic machinery itself. The Nazi bureaucracy became a racing doomsday machine, tirelessly dividing the sick from the healthy, fathers, mothers and children, absurdly and inhumanly separating people who should have remained together. Running on its own momentum, it realised every bureaucracy's dream: to manage a society of people more dead than alive. Against this bureaucracy of death, Schindler matched a bureaucracy of life: his own lists did not differentiate between men and women, workers and intellectuals, the able-bodied and the disabled in an ideal and fraternal society working for a totally unproductive business. Consequently, although the film dwells rather too much on the benevolence of Schindler – the only German employer to encourage his workers to celebrate Shabbat (!) – it nonetheless constitutes fascinating material about this little-known German resistance and the generosity of the man who saved so many of our fellows from a horrifying death.

The final procession of the descendants of "Schindler's Jews" past the grave of theman who has been given the epithet of "righteous" in Jerusalem is conclusive in this respect. As it stands, Spielberg's film is the tribute that a person of this stature deserved.

2. Modern historical reconstructions

Jon Avnet, *Uprising*

United States (2001), TV reconstruction, 177 min.; language: English

Historical theme: Warsaw Ghetto uprising

Moral theme: choice of a moral course of action in an immoral world

Aesthetic themes: historical reconstruction, realism, overstatement and mirror story

The director

Born in Brooklyn in 1949, Jon Avnet was the producer for a large number of films from 1976 onwards before moving into film direction with *Fried Green Tomatoes* (1991), which was a great success. *Uprising* is a television mini-series.

The film

1. Cast

Leelee Sobieski: Tosia Altman

Hank Azaria: Mordechai Anielewicz

David Schwimmer: Yitzhak Zuckerman

Jon Voight: Major General Jürgen Stroop

Donald Sutherland: Adam Czerniakow

Cary Elwes: Fritz Hippler

2. Background

1939: A dark year in Warsaw, where the Jews are beginning to bear the brunt of the invasion of Poland. Alarmed by Hitler's plans, the Jewish community endeavours to organise under the leadership of its most senior member, Adam Czerniakow. But increasingly draconian rules lead to over half a million individuals being confined to a small area of the city in appalling living conditions and the utmost discomfort. A young teacher, Mordechai Anielewicz, who has helped his students to escape to Palestine, is arrested and then returns in late 1940. He discovers the ghetto established by the Germans, with the Jews trapped there facing starvation, pestilence and deportation. After the large-scale round-ups of July to October 1942, Mordechai founds the ZOB (Jewish Fighting Organisation) with his friends and continues the struggle against the SS until April 1943, that is, right up to the final battle. This is the strictly, movingly and finely historical story told by Jon

Avnet, who surrounded himself with survivors of this final assault led by Major General Jürgen Stroop, such as Marek Edelman to write his screenplay.

3. Analysis

With the help of archival footage and a replica of the ghetto rebuilt in Bratislava, life inside the ghetto is meticulously reconstructed, with the terrible suffering inflicted on this community and the heroism of its final struggle. The result is a historically reliable and therefore very educational film which takes the audience through all the ins and outs of this tragic episode. This concern for exhaustiveness justifies the film's existence after so many other films about the Warsaw Ghetto, and the fact that it was made for television with a mini-series in mind explains its length (2 hours 57 minutes). But its length and its insistence on the bitter and moving nature of the situation are hard to bear. Is the history of the ghetto not sufficiently terrible in itself to stand without overstatement? This is the whole difference between cinema and television. The small screen requires the serial length in order to be exhaustive. In addition, it has so sated us with blood that it has become an insatiable Moloch, ever more avid for gory effects, whereas cinema, the art of ellipsis par excellence, has a moral code. Consequently, there arises yet again the question of realism in representation of the Shoah. Is it morally acceptable to portray anew, with ever greater technical perfection and ever finer colour images, the heaps of bodies, the ill-treatment endured and the cruelty of the Nazis? Perhaps it would be better to give young viewers a salutary shock by showing them authentic archival footage, thus introducing them to black-and-white silent cinema at the same time. It should be clearly specified whether the aim is documentary cinema or a historical reconstruction for entertainment purposes. Jon Avnet has tried to have it both ways. And the presence in the credits of Donald Sutherland and Jon Voight, excellent as they are, together with music by Maurice Jarre, tips the scales in favour of entertainment.

The film raises the ethical question of how a person in a position of responsibility can maintain moral order in the context of an immoral world. It illustrates two possible options, determined by different times and circumstances: that of Czerniakow, who, faced with the dilemma of protecting his people or resisting, decided to co-operate in order to reduce the risk run by his community, and that of Anielewicz, who, being much younger, chose armed resistance.

On the aesthetic level, the lengthy meditation on the power of cinema as a propaganda tool in which Avnet indulges by showing Fritz Hippler making his notorious film *The Eternal Jew* in the ghetto is too naive a mirror story or *mise en abyme*[41] to raise the standard of the film and, on the contrary, is likely to backfire. The scene in which Czerniakow is being filmed and the director asks him to gesticulate with his hands in order to look more Jewish is truly grotesque. However, it may be worth showing this historical film to students if you point out its weaknesses to them.

4. Teaching suggestions

This film is first and foremost a historical narrative which respects the chronological order of events. It can therefore be used in a history class. However, the teacher must draw attention to the perverse effects of this undeclared "cinema of entertainment", for in actual fact there is nothing more educational than a good film in which ellipsis opens up a field for explanation and discussion. *Uprising* overuses detailed reconstruction. Thus it would be a useful exercise to compare the excellent scene from Frédéric Rossif's *From Nuremberg to Nuremberg* in which Dr Korczak goes singing to the deportation train with his young charges, the scene from Andrzej Wajda's *Korczak*, and the sequence in *Uprising* which repeats the two others. The corpus effect, playing on the audience's memory, must be made clear to students, and it should be explained to them that this long and unnecessary scene could have been replaced by an emblematic citation which would have made the viewer curious enough to take a closer look.

---

41. The expression "*mise en abyme*", which in heraldry designates a small replica of the coat of arms located at its centre, was applied to literary criticism by the writer André Gide to refer to a setting or story which, within the main story, repeats the latter in miniature. "I find it pleasing when, in a work of art, you thus rediscover, transposed at the level of the characters, the subject of the work itself. Nothing better illuminates and more surely establishes the proportions of the whole. Thus in the pictures of Quentin Metsys, a small dark convex mirror reflects, in its turn, the interior of the room in which the action of the painting takes place." See on this subject Lucien Dallenbach, *The Mirror in the Text*, translated by Jeremy Whiteley with Emma Hughes (Chicago: University of Chicago Press; Cambridge: Polity Press, 1989).

3. "Simple reality"

Roman Polanski, *The Pianist*

United States (2002), historical fiction, 128 min.; language: English

Historical themes: life in the ghetto and a musician's survival thanks to a German music-lover

Moral theme: how to survive the death of one's entire family with the help of one's art

Aesthetic themes: historical reconstruction, realism, significant choices

The director

Born in Paris, Roman Polanski nevertheless spent his childhood in Poland. A survivor of the Krakow Ghetto, he lost his mother in the camps and was reunited with his father only after the war. This trauma and deprivation of affection were to leave their mark on his entire work. In the 1950s he went to the Łódź film school, where he made several short films. In 1962 he made his first full-length film *Knife in the Water*, which was nominated for a Best Foreign Language Film Academy Award. In Britain he made *Repulsion* (Silver Bear at the Berlin Film Festival in 1965), *Cul-de-Sac* (Golden Bear at Berlin in 1966) and *Dance of the Vampires* (1967). These critical and commercial successes enabled him to make his first Hollywood film, *Rosemary's Baby*, in 1968. The following year, after the murder of his wife, Sharon Tate, he returned to Europe to shoot *Macbeth*. His greatest public and critical success was *Chinatown* (which was nominated for eleven Oscars in 1974). In 1977 he made *Tess* (six Oscar nominations) in Europe as a tribute to his wife. In the 1980s and 1990s he made *Pirates*, *The Ninth Gate* and *Death and the Maiden* but without the success that he had enjoyed in the 1960s and 1970s.

There are some works that seem to be waiting for the right moment in their creator's life. Roman Polanski always knew that one day he would make a film about the war period in Poland. But at the same time he was reluctant because of two things he flatly rejected: autobiography and the Hollywood style of filming. Too modest for personal involvement and too rigorous to give in to American excesses, he therefore chose to adapt Wladyslaw Szpilman's novel *The Pianist* once he had discovered it. He was thus able to recall his memories and emotions by proxy, keeping his distance, and also to escape the absolute horror through a theme of hope: music as a means of survival.

The film

1. The cast

Adrien Brody: Wladyslaw Szpilman

Thomas Kretschmann: Captain Wilm Hosenfeld

Frank Finlay: Father

Maureen Lipman: Mother

Emilia Fox: Dorota

Ed Stoppard: Henryk

2. Background

A pianist for Polish radio, Wladyslaw Szpilman was considered a promising composer and a virtuoso pianist in 1939. Then, when his family was loaded into a freight wagon before his very eyes and he was pushed out of the line, he drifted from hiding-place to hiding-place for over two years, virtually without food, until he became a wild man, more dead than alive, who witnessed the ghetto's uprising. His memoirs, which he wrote in 1946 under the title *Death of a City* were reissued by his son in 1998 as *The Pianist*.

3. Analysis

Roman Polanski has chosen historical reconstruction to portray these recollections and hired a little-known American actor, Adrien Brody, together with the Polish pianist Janusz Olejniczak. He entrusted set design to Allan Starski and costumes to Anna Sheppard, both of whom had worked with Spielberg on *Schindler's List*. An irony of fate: the production designer reconstructed the city at the Babelsberg studios in Berlin, redesigning a residential area of Potsdam and the Praga district in Warsaw. Right at the opening of the film, we are shown a sequence of the streets of Warsaw in 1939 in black-and-white as if to warn us that the film-maker expects no indulgence. The colour tone will subsequently be skilfully adjusted to convey the slow escalation of horror in such a peaceful city: threats, compulsory wearing of the white armband with the blue star, establishment of the ghetto, ever more indiscriminate killing, mass deportation and systematic extermination.

However, distancing himself from Hollywood style, Polanski strives to adopt the most objective tone possible to match the cool and detached description of events that is so striking in the novel. It is doubtless for this reason that he discards the autobiographical narrative and forgoes the voice-over that would seem the obvious choice. The director's aim is to make the viewer a powerless witness, whom he incites to revolt. What he emphasises is the random nature of the discrimination that results in summary executions in the open street and the fact that the Germans treat the Jews like animals, separating them at a glance, driving them along and slaughtering them without a second thought. Their arbitrary choices have clearly been sensed as a savage destruction of his illusions by the horrified child that Polanski uncovers in himself and through whose eyes we see the story. He now realises how far survival was a matter of pure chance and incredible luck in such conditions. If the Jews nevertheless hoped for the best, it was firstly because they could not imagine what awaited them and secondly because they retained their faith in human nature despite the barbarity they saw unfolding before their very eyes.

Wladyslaw Szpilman had an additional reason to hope: music. A pianist for Polish radio, he was a bright hope for Polish music. Music was his life. *The Pianist* is a deeply moving film which plunges us into barbarism and decline before giving us one tiny ray of hope. A witness and plaything of history like Polanski himself, Szpilman, played here by Adrien Brody in the title role, brilliantly conveys the moral and physical degeneration of a fine musician reduced to a state of savagery by an inhuman system: Adrien Brody communicates helpless despair and indignation with noteworthy restraint, no doubt required by the director. We may have our reservations about this umpteenth reconstruction, but the director's talent immediately puts it head and shoulders above all the others. Rejection of virtuosity and complacency, pent-up emotion and an absence of pathos conspire to bring out the sensibility of the martyred musician. Far from any overstatement, the concern for authenticity has been motivated solely by a concern "to show things the way they were, no more, no less", so as to provide information for the youngest viewers whilst emphasising, through this true story, that men are as frail as they are strong. The "thinking reed" is also a creative creature whom art can save from despair.

4. Teaching suggestions

It is a good idea to have students read Wladyslaw Szpilman's admirable book in order that they may compare the written style with the cinematic style, indicating the equivalents that the director has used to translate Szpilman's detachment and certain turns of phrase which are almost humorous.

It would be appropriate to play students Chopin's Nocturne in C sharp minor, Opus 27, No. 1 and point out that, being Polish and also an exile, Chopin was the obvious choice for Polanski when he was looking for the music for his film: a mournful expression of the misfortunes of a martyred people. Neither illustrative nor ornamental, it matches the narrator's distressed state of mind.

As for the *mise en scène*, you might compare a sequence from *Uprising* with a sequence from *The Pianist* to indicate the difference between each director's choices: overstatement and understatement. In *The Pianist* the tight narrative is illustrated by images that are fleeting but no less striking: the old man in the wheelchair being thrown out of the window, the family sharing the caramel, the workers being killed.

4. Aftermath of war

Alan J. Pakula, *Sophie's Choice*

United States (1982), fiction, 150 min., colour; language: English; based on the novel by W. Styron; cinematography: Nestor Almendros

Historical theme: complexity of the situation in the camps

Moral theme: survival after the Shoah

Aesthetic themes: historical reconstruction, flashback

The director

Born in 1928, Alan J. Pakula began his career as a producer before making *Pookie* (1969), *Klute* (1971), *The Parallax View* (1974), *All the President's Men* (1976) and *Rollover* (1981). *Sophie's Choice* was his ninth film.

The film

1. Cast

Meryl Streep: Sophie Zawistowski

Kevin Kline: Nathan

Peter MacNicol: Stingo

Rita Karin: Yetta

Stephen D. Newman: Larry

2. Background

Bowled over by William Styron's novel, Alan J. Pakula decided to film the story of Sophie, an Auschwitz survivor (Polish but not Jewish) who meets the novice writer Stingo in Brooklyn in 1947. Stingo (the story's narrator), Sophie and her lover (the Jewish intellectual Nathan Landau) soon become inseparable, both men being in love with Sophie, who makes Stingo her confidant. He discovers that their love for each other brings with it terrible suffering, for which he seeks the reasons. Gradually delving into their past, he understands why: Sophie is consumed with remorse for having managed to survive her children, dead in Auschwitz, and Nathan, an American Jew, suffers from not having had any role in that dark period – a twofold guilt which is wearing them down. Both seek oblivion in music and unbridled sex. This chronicle of intellectual life in New York in the post-war years shows young people branded by what they have experienced.

3. Analysis

The film, like the novel, deals with a painful theme: the return to life after internment in a camp. Sophie, traumatised and suffering in the flesh, embodies this difficulty (which Stingo finds hard to understand) with the utmost charm – conveyed in the performance of Meryl Streep, who was awarded an Oscar for best actress in 1983. The historical reconstruction is more of New York than the camps. Footage of the latter makes a fleeting appearance, in black-and-white flashback, interrupting the present-day colour narrative, thus following a well-established stylistic technique introduced by Alain Resnais. This is perhaps what made the film a success. The extermination remains subliminal like an unendurable burden on everyone's memory and subconscious. Sophie's craving for love is therefore not only a feature of her character but also arises from the need to mend the mental and physical wounds left by her internment.

4. Teaching suggestions

The emotion aroused by this film should not lead us to neglect analysis. The issues to be addressed are historical: the complexity of the situation in the camps, in which Jews and non-Jews from across Europe co-existed; and the cruelty of the SS, who forced Sophie to make an impossible choice between her children. But there are also cinematic issues: the flashback technique, the alternation between black-and-white and colour, the inclusion of archival material in the fiction, and the historical reconstruction of post-war New York. Students should be encouraged to find connections between these two aspects and the choices made in translating the historical elements into images.

Istvan Szabo, *Taking Sides*

Britain/France/Germany/Austria (2001), historical fiction, 108 min., colour; language: English

Historical theme: aftermath of war in occupied Germany

Moral theme: the choice to be made by an artist under an iniquitous regime

Aesthetic themes: historical reconstruction, realism, investigation

The director

Born in Budapest in 1938, Istvan Szabo is a very great Hungarian film-maker. He has specialised in grand historical frescoes dealing with crucial human problems against a background of crisis or war. We may mention *Mephisto* (1981), *Colonel Redl* (1985), *Hanussen* (1988) and *Sunshine* (1999).

The film

1. Cast

Harvey Keitel: Major Steve Arnold

Moritz Bleibtreu: Lieutenant David Wills

Stellan Skarsgård: Wilhelm Furtwängler

Birgit Minichmayr: Emmi Straube

2. Background

In a Berlin in ruins in which the Allies have begun to hunt down Nazis, Major Steve Arnold is put in charge of an inquiry into the past of Wilhelm Furtwängler, the great orchestral conductor, who is suspected of having belonged to the Nazi party. While questioning all the musicians in the orchestra and searching through the files, Arnold becomes convinced that Furtwängler actively sympathised with Hitler and does not let go until he has secured at least a partial condemnation of the man.

3. Analysis

The film's great merit is that it raises a moral problem broader than that of tracking down the culprits: the position to be adopted by civilians in wartime. Moreover, in this case the civilian in question is a very great artist of an enemy country, while the American bent on getting to the bottom of Nazi machinations embodies a civilisation which is the opposite extreme from German culture. Ignorant of classical music, he is familiar only with the swing sung and danced by his country's army and needs the active help of his two assistants – a young German

Jew whose parents were deported, and a young Berlin woman whose father took part in the officers' plot against Hitler – to introduce him to Beethoven. This being so, is he capable of understanding the frame of mind of a great musician who claims to be able to separate art from politics and be concerned only with pursuing his career, deemed more important to the world than the Nazi crimes of which he had no knowledge? Is not the investigator, uncompromising as to the principle, in the process of depriving eternal, universal culture of one of its geniuses? But Furtwängler has a way of defending himself which is self-accusatory, and Arnold has an unanswerable reply to his arguments: Furtwängler himself said that he had saved Jews, but if he knew nothing about the "final solution", why did he think that Jews needed to be saved?

The *mise en scène*, although very theatrical, is especially effective. Szabo stages with matchless talent the confrontation between Harvey Keitel (Arnold), a claim adjuster willing to use the dirtiest of tricks to show up a man he believes to be guilty, and Stellan Skarsgård (Furtwängler), a tormented artist, whose greatness and pettinesses he exposes at the same time. In an increasingly claustrophobic drama behind closed doors the two characters clash and reveal themselves. To avoid any Manichaeism, Szabo shows the reservations of Arnold's two assistants as to his methods, and unsettles us, before persuading us of the unpardonable nature of any involvement – even intellectual – in genocide. He thus personifies the clash between two civilisations and two cultures, old Europe and new America, but not between two moral codes. For morality is unique and universal, including for artists, who in his opinion have no excuse for collaborating. While Furtwängler was able to continue his career in Germany, he was banned from giving concerts in the United States.

4. Teaching suggestions

An analysis of differences in class, social background and culture between the two protagonists should lead on to an interesting discussion of the position to be adopted in such an exceptional case: should the artist be saved despite his collaboration (intellectual at any rate) with the Nazi regime, or should he suffer the fate of an ordinary war criminal.

PART THREE
EUROPEAN FICTION FILMS

1. Nazi propaganda

Veit Harlan, *Jud Süss (Jew Süss)*

Germany (1940), 98 min.; language: German

Historical theme: Nazi propaganda about Jews

The director

Veit Harlan was a German film director who was born in Berlin in 1899 and died in Capri in 1964. Initially an actor and theatre producer, he subsequently became a mouthpiece for Nazi ideology (*Jew Süss*, 1940; *The Great King*, 1941; *Burning Hearts*, 1945). He also made some romantic films (*Immensee*, 1943) and exotic films (*Stars over Colombo*, 1953-54).

The film

1. Cast

Ferdinand Marian: Joseph Süss Oppenheimer

Werner Krauss: Rabbi Loew, Levi

Heinrich George: Karl Alexander, Duke of Württemberg

Kristina Söderbaum: Dorothea, Sturm's daughter

Eugen Klöpfer: Sturm

2. Background

The film tells of the relations between Karl Alexander, Duke of Württemberg and his Jewish financier Joseph Süss Oppenheimer. Süss was born at the beginning of the 18th century in Heidelberg. Probably the natural child of a Christian field officer, he lived on the fringe of the Jewish community, which explains why he became the duke's financial adviser. He was a court Jew with a tragic destiny, who, after having made the fortune of a greedy tyrant, was condemned to death and publicly executed for having seduced a maidservant of German blood. His story has become a legend, handed down by various works of fiction and even some historical works, both anti-Semitic and Jewish, including the novel and play by the German Jew Lion Feuchtwanger (1925).

3. Analysis

Nazi cinema understood the importance of film propaganda. In particular, it commissioned Fritz Hippler to make *The Eternal Jew*, which characterised Jews as capitalists, Bolsheviks and foreigners all at the same time, Leni Riefenstahl to shoot her film about the Munich Games, and other works in the same style. In addition, Joseph Goebbels, Minister of Culture and Propaganda in the Third Reich, asked Veit Harlan to exploit the potential of the historical figure Joseph Süss Oppenheimer, who had lived in Württemberg in the early 18th century. It was this remarkable figure who thus inspired the director to make the film *Jew Süss*, where some of the crimes attributed to the central character are designed to justify the anti-Jewish measures taken by the government of the Third Reich. The film was completed in 1940. It begins as a comedy of manners and ends with an insistent appeal to eliminate the Jews. With the help of a large budget, good actors, and excellent technical staff provided by Goebbels, Harlan had the task of responding to Chaplin's *The Great Dictator* with a counter-offensive worthy of the name. Mixing together the traditional themes of anti-Semitism (sex, money and conspiracy), the film was presented at the Venice Film Festival and was acclaimed in his reviews by the young Michelangelo Antonioni as "incisive", "entertaining" and "intelligent". This widely distributed Nazi propaganda film was a great success with the public, attracting some 20 million cinemagoers throughout Europe, 8 million of whom were in Germany and 1 million in France alone. Admittedly, the film was booed on various occasions, but it excited a great wave of curiosity. And it became a key argument in support of the "final solution". As for Veit Harlan, spared by de-Nazification, he was acquitted at his two trials and was able to end his days peacefully in Capri.

4. Teaching suggestions

The purpose of such a work, as Claude Singer explains in his book *Le Juif Süss et la propagande nazie, l'histoire confisquée* (Les Belles lettres, 2003), is to misappropriate a historical figure and exalt Germany's romantic past, but also to rewrite this past by denigrating Jews for the requirements of the Nazi cause. To this end German directors such as Leni Riefenstahl, conscious of the close connection between aesthetics, ethics and politics, deployed the full resources of their art. You might show how Veit Harlan has tried to portray the Jew as a sexual pervert and has accused him of conspiracy, of pursuing power and of cupidity. For ideological purposes he has thus used extreme close-ups, violent light contrasts, editing, and, in particular, dissolves and shot/reverse-shot so as to lend maximum conviction to what he has to say. This expressionism is intended to turn the Jew into a terrifying monster and exacerbate feelings of hatred towards him. More specifically, as ClaudeSinger has shown, he copies the structure of Murnau's film *Nosferatu*, making the bridge-crossing scene the turning point which suggests the comparison between the Jew with the claw-like hands and the vampire thirsting for blood. We can thus gauge cinema's tendency to produce effects which alter perceptions and play with the imagination. It became a formidable weapon in the hands of people such as Harlan.

2. Historical reconstructions

Heinz Schirk, *Die Wannseekonferenz (The Wannsee Conference)*

West Germany/Austria (1984), 85 min., colour; language: German/Latin

Historical theme: practical organisation of the "final solution"

Moral themes: how to expunge millions of human beings at a stroke of the pen, the discreet language of barbarism

Aesthetic theme: meticulous and uncompromising historical reconstruction

The director

Heinz Schirk is a television director who attempted to apply the "docudrama" method to the most difficult of subjects. His meticulous reconstruction of the material details of the day forms part of this approach, but it also takes on a very different meaning because of the substance of the decisions taken on that day. Coming in the midst of a debate about German guilt, his film, by its historical rigour, indicates a genuine determination in Germany and Austria to stop averting their eyes and to accept a past whose memory should help them avoid making the same mistakes. This is an educational and cathartic project which makes memory the precondition for a different future.

The film

1. Cast

Robert Atzorn: Hofmann

Friedrich G. Beckhaus: Müller

Gerd Böckmann: Eichmann

Jochen Busse: Leibbrandt

Hans-Werner Bussinger: Luther

Dietrich Mattausch: Heydrich

2. Background

This film adopts the guise of fiction although it is based on sound research. It reconstructs in real time the course of the meeting organised by Heydrich on 20 January 1942 in the Berlin suburbs between Nazi political and military leaders (including Eichmann, Müller, Freisler and Stuckart), a meeting of evil memory, in which the practical arrangements for implementing the "final solution" were decided. The film is based on shorthand notes and on the official minutes of the conference drawn up by Eichmann himself (of which only thirty copies were distributed), as well as on Eichmann's evidence at his trial.

3. Analysis

Set in a pleasant house in the suburbs of Berlin, the film portrays a meeting that is more social than political. The film's strength lies in the accuracy of the details and a *mise en scène* which endeavours to convey the "soft" side of this afternoon during which the fate of thousands was calmly decided behind closed doors over cups of tea and glasses of brandy. It allows us to put polite and smiling faces to acts whilst a distance is maintained between characters and camera. The courteous attitudes, euphemistic language and obedience of future executants such as Eichmann are chilling (it is worth comparing the scenes in which he features with clips from *The Specialist* by Rony Brauman and Eyal Sivan). The workings of this collective crime are personified by human beings who like everyone else, are preoccupied with their mental and physical comfort. Triteness and pettiness, cowardice and unscrupulousness, an absurd concern with the details of the implementation procedure, and the abjectness of the compromises are what emerge from this meeting. The grotesque is combined with the hideous, as in Jarry or Kafka. Monstrosity takes on its most banal aspect. The second part of the film, given over to endless discussions about whether to exterminate "half Jews" "quarter Jews", etc., shows these men attaining new heights of imbecilic cynicism. This polished *mise en scène*, which plays on understatement, is more effective than any scenes of slaughter. It dissects the workings of the horror and shows the calm human face of barbarism, thus encouraging us to reflect on the ease with which politicians, either through ambition or through cowardice, can slide from power into abuse of power at the expense of the people they are governing.

4. Teaching suggestions

Dominique Chansel stresses that the film must be seen in the context of the intellectual debate that was going on in Germany in the 1970s and 1980s on the Germans' responsibility for the "final solution". Anxious to make a thorough historical study of this subject, certain intellectuals influenced the director's declared intention of "compiling a file for the future". Hence the hybrid form of this "docudrama",[42] which tells us, once again, as much about the period when it was made as about the past it portrays.

This reconstruction is particularly interesting for its strictly historical aspect and its way of revealing what went on behind the scenes in Nazi history. It allows precise documentary work on the chronology and the practical measures planned through a comparison between the acts referred to in the film and actual historical events. You might start a discussion about the use of language as a means of window

---

42. Dominique Chansel, op. cit., p. 213.

dressing the reality in question and analyse the choices relating to the *mise en scène* (actors, set, properties, stage business) and to the point of view adopted. But it should be pointed out that this is a reconstruction and not a documentary and that Raul Hilberg, an expert on Nazi bureaucracy, fiercely attacked this film, which nevertheless took certain liberties with the historical facts, in the *New York Times*. Everybody knows that you should never count on absolute historical accuracy in the cinema.

Andrzej Wajda, *Korczak*

Poland (1990), historical reconstruction, 115 min., black-and-white; language: English

Historical theme: life in the Warsaw Ghetto

Moral theme: choice of a moral course of action in an immoral world

Aesthetic themes: historical reconstruction, realism

The director

Born in Poland in 1926, Andrzej Wajda had to interrupt his studies on the death of his father, a cavalry officer called up to the German border. He himself was a liaison officer for the Polish government in exile. He resumed his studies in 1946 and was enrolled "by accident" in the national film school in Lodz. Films such as *Ashes and Diamonds*, *Landscape after the Battle*, *Man of Marble* and *Danton* quickly became international successes.

The film

1. Cast

Wojtek Pszoniak: Janusz Korczak

Ewa Dalkowska: Stefa

Piotr Kozlowski: Heniek

Marzena Trybala: Estera

2. Background

Wajda tells the true story of Janusz Korczak, an eminent Polish-Jewish paediatrician, writer and educator, who spent the last two years of his life in the Warsaw Ghetto with two hundred orphans, for whom he was caring at the risk of his life, before being taken away with them to the camp at Treblinka and the gas chamber. Agnieszka Holland's screenplay is based on his diary. For the director, this is both a tribute to an exceptional man and a testimony to combat oblivion.

3. Analysis

Wajda had already exposed his compatriots' anti-Semitism in *Samson* (1961), a rather awkward transposition of the Bible story to Poland in 1934-35. The character Jakub Gold reveals himself to be a Jew upon entering university, commits a criminal act and is sent to prison. Released with the outbreak of war, he lives in the ghetto, where, betrayed by a woman, he remains hidden in a cellar during the uprising before blowing himself up together with the insurgents' printing press during the final SS assault on the ghetto.

Holding any aesthetic or melodramatic ambitions to be out of place, Wajda once again chose to film *Korczak* in black-and-white, which he felt was better suited to his subject. According to Wajda, it is much easier to depict evil and evil-doers than a saint such as Korczak. What interested him in this extraordinary character was his struggle against his own weakness. Wojtek Pszoniak's performance as the doctor is remarkable.

Furthermore, all Jewish themes had been virtually banished from Polish culture, and the film-maker thought it time to portray the atmosphere of the ghetto and the extermination of the Jews in the cinema. However, the film gave rise to fierce controversy for two reasons.

Firstly, it was suspected of anti-Semitism because Wajda showed the existence of Jewish cabarets and black marketeers inside the ghetto but not a hint of any anti-Semites, which is perfectly understandable in the context of the ghetto, where there were only Jews. Did Wajda really want to sully the Jews and rehabilitate the Poles? The claim is absurd. We know that the tendency of eyewitnesses and survivors to consider the Jews irreproachable corresponds to a period of delusional sanctimoniousness subsequently denounced by Marek Edelman himself.

Secondly, Wajda has been accused of promoting revisionism and denial with his final, very dreamlike, sequence in which the children, just as they are being led to their deaths, seem to rise into the sky in a haze. Lanzmann interpreted this as a desire to console the viewers with a dissolve which was, in his opinion, an aesthetic appropriation of the destruction of the Jews. This is a great exaggeration.

Can we really believe all this? In doing so, we would be underrating a great film-maker as well as underestimating the audience's imagination and disregarding the very nature of cinema, which is first and foremost an art and above all an art of ellipsis designed precisely to exercise the audience's imagination. Robby Muller's cinematography also has much to do with the success of the project.

4. Teaching suggestions

We are more accustomed to dreamlike atmospheres now than when the film came out, and the true fate of Dr Korczak's children will be clear to everyone. You could get students to work on the question of pathos and representation whilst drawing their attention to what may be deemed certain excesses in the hospital scenes but encouraging them to appreciate a very fine and dignified ending, which they will judge at its true value.

3. History and fiction

Andrzej Munk, *Pasazerka (The Passenger)*

Poland (1963), 75 min., black-and-white; language: Polish

Historical theme: life in the camps

Philosophical theme: repressed memory

Aesthetic themes: reconstructing memories, bad faith

The director

Born in 1921, Andrzej Munk was highly traumatised by the war. After studying architecture and law in Warsaw and then film directing at the Lodz film school, he worked in Polish television news. Together with Andrzej Wajda, he personified the revival of Polish cinema struggling against Soviet bureaucracy. Nevertheless, he had a lot of admiration for Eisenstein and the early cinema of the USSR. One of his previous films *The Men of Blue Cross* (*Blekitny krzyz*, 1955) also dealt with war.

The film

1. Cast

Aleksandra Slaska: Liza

Anna Ciepielewska: Marta

Jan Kreczmar: Marta's fiancé

2. Background

A German woman on a transatlantic liner imagines that she recognises a former prisoner from Auschwitz who had been under her authority. She recalls her memories for her husband, but the truth which gradually emerges is not the same as what she tells him.

3. Analysis

A transatlantic liner is "a floating island in time". It is these words in the voice-over which open the film, whose initial shots are static: two women looking at each other, and an uncomprehending husband. The film is unfinished, gaining additional depth from its incompleteness, for we are immediately confronted with three patterns of shooting: static shots; silent moving sequences composed of long shots depicting life in the camp; and moving sequences with sound – either dialogue or narrative voice-over – which recount the relationship between the two women. The film is meant to be a psychological and psychoanalytical study of the mental world of a person who gradually discovers the pleasure of power. The fact that this person is a woman adds further interest to the study.

In fact, we are presented with two subtly different stories in flashback: the watered-down story told to the husband about how Liza "facilitated" Marta's life in the camp, and the story of actual events, which portrays a relationship that is much more ambiguous and debatable. In one story Liza is "doing her duty", lightening the prisoners' burden, and maintains a special relationship with Marta, having made her her assistant and even taken on her fiancé in order that he may be closer to her and look after her when she is ill: images that have been carefully sanitised and rendered innocuous. However, in the second story, consisting of memories which Liza recalls from deep inside, things are much harsher. Liza's true feelings about Marta are, to begin with, jealousy of her life and her fiancé's unstinting love for her and a refusal of any complicity with this couple who cast back to her the image of her own solitude. Then she gradually becomes intoxicated with the discovery that she can wield power over them: "I wanted to let her know that I could give her Taddeusz like you give a sweet to a well-behaved child." If she saves her life and allows her to see her fiancé, it is so that Marta may understand what she owes to Liza and the latter may receive her gratitude and even her trust. But Marta, taking refuge in a silence undoubtedly intended by the director, resists her overtures. She has a countenance that is more expressive than any words. In the key scene where, suffering from disease, she is questioned by Red Cross inspectors and cannot speak on pain of reprisal, she has the look of a hunted animal at bay. The scene in which she reads an invented love letter in the place of a note containing names and numbers of SS officers, on the other hand, gives free rein to lyricism. And there is also the superb scene where the prisoners are listening to a concert given by some of their number and where the violin is drowned by the whistling and rumbling of the trains; the two lovers silently try to draw near to one another at the risk of their lives for a moment of unforgettable intensity.

4. Teaching suggestions

These scenes should be studied closely to demonstrate that this is an imposing film not because it shows life in a camp, although it was the first to do so, but because its intention is to lift the problem of power and resistance onto a universal plane. The camp becomes a symbol for all fascist or repressive systems which endeavour to subjugate not only the human body but also the human mind – systems represented by people weak enough to yield to the temptation of sadism. Some exceptional beings such as Marta manage to hold out against the path of masochism through their unshakeable self-respect. This is the eternal dialectic of master and slave, which loses its object if the slave, although ill-treated and put to death, rejects his status and asserts that of a full human being even in the worst conditions. Does not this conflict, which goes much deeper than the bald historical reconstruction, make clear the very essence of the concentration camp system, which tried to reduce men to the level of animals? Other films, such as Joseph Losey's *The Servant* and Liliana Cavanni's *The Night Porter*, have explored the complex relationship between master and slave, torturer and victim, which does not rule out a degree of fascination. But, apart from the fact that it was the first to attempt such a portrayal, the film has the distinctive feature of establishing this relationship between two women and studying the psychology of the overseer whilst leaving that of the prisoner impenetrable or at least allowing it to be inferred from her acts alone.

Joseph Losey, *Monsieur Klein (Mr Klein)*

France/Italy (1976), historical fiction, 123 min., colour; language: French

Historical theme: occupied France and collaboration

Philosophical theme: vertigo of identity

Aesthetic themes: historical reconstruction, challenging realism, an investigation

The director

This great American director belonged to an important family in Wisconsin. Born in 1909, Joseph Losey studied philosophy, medicine and English literature in America but was above all interested in theatre and managed to work with Bertolt Brecht, whose *Galileo* he staged in 1947 with Charles Laughton. His first feature, *The Boy with Green Hair*, was acclaimed as a masterpiece in 1948. But during shooting of *The Prowler* in Italy in 1951 he was served with a subpoena by the House Un-American Activities Committee and decided to go into exile in Britain. There he worked with Harold Pinter. But he also turned out second-rate films until 1963, the year of his most impressive work, *The Servant*. *Accident* (1967) and *The Go-Between* (1971) put him among the best directors of his generation. After a further series of unremarkable films he made *Mr Klein* (1976), a genuine masterpiece, and a memorable version of *Don Giovanni* (1979). His last film was *Steaming*, based on the play by Nell Dunn and released posthumously in 1985, since the director died in 1984.

The film

1. Cast

Alain Delon: Robert Klein

Jeanne Moreau: Florence

Juliet Berto: Janine

Suzanne Flon: The concierge

Michael Lonsdale: Pierre

2. Background

In 1942 occupied Paris, Robert Klein leads a hedonistic existence and is growing rich by purchasing the property of desperate Jews. When he finds on his doorstep a copy of the local Jewish newspaper, which seems to consider him a subscriber, he discovers the existence of another Robert Klein, who is a Jewish member of the Resistance. He starts investigating this double, initially to prove that he himself is not a member of the Jewish community, but then gradually becomes fascinated by this character who is braver and more enigmatic than himself.

3. Analysis

Franco Solinas's Kafkaesque script creates a disturbing atmosphere. The film's opening shots take us to a doctor's surgery where a doctor is roughly examining a woman in order to determine to which race she belongs. The close-up has a scientific purpose, since it serves to emphasise how human beings are treated like animals (later Klein will be described as a vulture and then as a horse), and a political purpose, since it straight away characterises the atmosphere of Vichy France. This scene is in stark contrast to the voluptuous atmosphere in Klein's bedroom, where his mistress is lounging in bed. The scene in which he buys the Dutch painting marks him out as a profiteer and incidentally introduces the theme of Jewish origins.

The interest of the film lies in the slow process whereby Robert Klein comes to identify with his namesake. Little by little, the idle and high-living aesthete slips into the other man's shoes as if he were ashamed of his own life. Trains play a decisive part in this metamorphosis, as does the violently anti-Semitic scene (a mirror of the plot) which he witnesses at a nightclub. Once the caricaturing of Jews is felt to be unbearable, the identification process has started. The name is the crux of the plot, as it is for Kafka's characters, whose initial the scriptwriter has borrowed. It is both a symbol of the arbitrariness of the political system and the locus of a hazy, vacillating and problematic identity that allows room for a different identity freely chosen and assumed. From the round of women's forenames – as interchangeable as their persons for the pleasure seeker – there emerges the surname of a being who is not yet a man but who will eventually become one owing to a dangerous and providential mistake. This identity, initially a legal identity, becomes the pretext for every kind of primal fantasy and primitive scene. Consumed by intrinsic doubt and the vertigo of identity, in search of his real self, and aware of the mismatch between his name and his character, Mr Klein – egoism personified – symbolically boards a train to leave behind his country, his identity and his mask. But an unknown force brings him back again, and he is reunited with his name just at the time when "Aryan" certificates are being duly introduced. The buses of the Vélodrome d'Hiver round-up take him inexorably to the fate that he has chosen, in a train where he symbolically meets again the Jew from whom he had bought the painting.

4. Teaching suggestions

Since the film is too clever to fall into the trap of clumsy historical denunciation, students might be asked to note all the fleeting signs of the political situation in occupied France: the medical examinations, queues at grocer's shops, the key role of concierges, the police planning for the route of the buses to the Vélodrome d'Hiver, the yellow star reflected in the bus window. The film should be studied as a demonstration of the risks run by identity in a period of dictatorship and collaboration and as a labyrinthine journey through the tortuous paths of a police state while the population, taken hostage, plays its role of the passive and silent majority.

Other points worth studying are the suspense leading up to the moment when all is revealed – except for the character's identity, which is disclosed too late to save him from a suicidal destiny – and, above all, the semi-fantastic aspect of this gradual vampirising of an individual by an imaginary character whom he finds more interesting and prestigious than himself. The Resistance fighter first conveys a sense of romanticism before revealing to the dandy the vacuity of his own existence, fascinating him and invading his life. This is a philosophical and metaphysical film about the aberrations of a political system, the impossibility of remaining uninvolved and the madness of having to forfeit the self when the ego has suffered a narcissistic wound and is losing all respect for itself. Gerry Fisher's cinematography is reminiscent of Edmond Richard's in Orson Welles' *The Trial*, while the choice of Suzanne Flon, who acted in the latter film, bears out this affinity.

Louis Malle, *Au revoir les enfants (Goodbye, Children)*

France (1987), 104 min., colour; language: French

Historical theme: occupied France

Aesthetic theme: reconstructing childhood memories

The director

Born in Thumeries (France) in 1932, Louis Malle is one of the least controversial representatives of the French New Wave. The son of wealthy industrialists, he first studied political science at the Sorbonne before enrolling at the French film school IDHEC. An assistant to Jacques Cousteau on his film *The Silent World* (1956) and then in the same year to Robert Bresson on *A Man Escaped*, he made his first film, *Lift to the Scaffold* (1957), with Jeanne Moreau, whom he directed the following year in *The Lovers*, a film which created a scandal because of the eroticism of its superb cinematography. There followed *Zazie dans le métro* (1960), *A Very Private Affair* (1961), *A Time to Live and a Time to Die* (1963), *Dearest Love* (1971), *Lacombe Lucien* (1974), *Pretty Baby* (1978) and *Atlantic City* (1980). Louis Malle always retained his love of documentary. He alternated it with fiction, making films such as *And the Pursuit of Happiness* and *Vanya on 42nd Street* or making films halfway between fiction and documentary, such as *Alamo Bay* (1985). He died in Beverly Hills in 1995.

The film

1. Cast

Gaspard Manesse: Julien

Raphael Fejtö: Bonnet

Francine Racette: Mme Quentin

Philippe Morier-Genoud: Father Jean

François Berléand: Father Michel

2. Background

An eleven-year-old boy in a Catholic boarding school strikes up a friendship with one of his fellow students to whom he is attracted because he finds him different from the others, until he realises that he is Jewish.

3. Analysis

After a long exile in the United States, Louis Malle returned to France with this autobiographical film about his childhood. The director of *Lacombe Lucien* (which analysed the process whereby a farmer's son who is completely apolitical comes to be enlisted in the Vichy militia) recalls his schooldays at a Catholic school and his friendship with a Jewish boy who was being hidden by the priests at the risk of their lives. Perhaps it was to that freezing morning in 1944 when, in the Carmelite school in Avon, near Fontainebleau, the Germans came looking for his friend and took him away before his very eyes, that he owed his cinematic calling. All his work, vibrant with generosity and devoted to the cause of the downtrodden, seems to be rooted in this obsessive memory, which he here attempts to exorcise.

With great sensitivity Malle uses small touches to depict the bonds which gradually develop between these two boys in the often harsh world of the school. His portrayal is a model of restraint, showing the nature of the child he once was – shy, withdrawn and too attached to his mother (had he already depicted himself in *Dearest Love*?). The cruel absurdity of the world is exposed, and a vocation to help the downtrodden – a source of constant inspiration – is awakened, while conformity is denounced and a determination to understand minorities is evinced.

The cinematography of Renato Berta lends this film its special atmosphere of a bygone age which owes less to history than to childhood memories. The Sainte-Croix school, with its students clad in navy-blue capes with their crew-cuts and Basque berets, playing at walking on stilts to warm themselves up, and above all the cold light of this winter in the Ile-de-France countryside makes for an almost dreamlike ambiance, or at any rate one which conveys the distortions produced in objective reality by a child's memory.

4. Teaching suggestions

All teenagers will share the emotion felt by Louis Malle in this extremely personal film. He is trying to convey to them his view of the world and show them the brutal destruction of the paradise that is childhood. The adult world is, to begin with, the pain of being separated from a mother who is so loving but so distant and the violence of an everyday life to which the spoilt child is not accustomed. But it is above all the war, which enters this calm provincial school, which seems so well protected, without any warning. It is also the maturity acquired through the abrupt severance of a beautiful friendship and the revelation of Father Jean's heroic role.

Francesco Rosi, *La Tregua (The Truce)*

*Italy/France/Germany/Switzerland (1997), 125 min., colour, based on
Primo Levi's autobiography of the same name; languages: English, Russian,
German, Polish, Italian and Latin*

Historical theme: camp inmates' return to life

Moral theme: how to bear new trials after those already suffered

Aesthetic theme: historical reconstruction

The director

Francesco Rosi, one of the greatest Italian directors, was born on 15 November 1922 in Naples. His films are essentially political and literary, inspired by incidents that have influenced the life of his country, such as *Hands Over the City* (1963), *The Mattei Affair* (1971), *Lucky Luciano* (1973) and *Illustrious Corpses* (1975), and superb adaptations of major works of literature such as *Christ Stopped at Eboli* (1979), *Chronicle of a Death Foretold* (1986) and *The Palermo Connection* (1989).

The film

1. Cast

John Turturro: Primo Levi

Rade Serbedzija: The Greek

Massimo Ghini: Cesare

Stefano Dionisi: Daniele

Teco Celio: Colonel Rovi

Claudio Bisio: Ferrari

2. Background

Primo Levi's second work, published in 1963, recounts the odyssey of his return from Auschwitz: from the Soviet troops' entry into the camp to his long trek home, via the USSR, to Turin.

3. Analysis

Adapting this story for the cinema was a challenge since the strength of the text lies in the writing, which is precise, meticulous and sometimes ironic but never garrulous or self-pitying. Encouraged by Primo Levi himself, Francesco Rosi took up this challenge. If, at 75, he wanted to tackle such a subject, it was to educate young people. This is probably why his film somewhat lacks force. For Levi's humour and entomological precision he substitutes a rather caricatured depiction of the characters, a distinct tendency to melodrama, and the misplaced lyricism of Luis Bacalov's music. The performances are nevertheless remarkable. John Turturro, who received the Best Actor award at Cannes in 1991 for his role in *Barton Fink* by Joel and Ethan Cohen, plays the writer brilliantly. Emaciated, with burning eyes, he gives a sensitive rendering of a role that is "impossible", in his own words, and all the more difficult because the character is primarily an observer. It is highly unfortunate that Francesco Rosi thought fit to add a scene of his own to the text, in which a German prisoner kneels before the former camp inmate who shows him his yellow star. Yet Primo Levi wrote: "Nobody looked us in the eye, nobody would talk to us; they were deaf, blind and dumb, imprisoned in their ruins as in a fortress of wilful ignorance, still strong and capable of hatred, still prisoners of their old tangle of pride and guilt." Does this amount to betrayal? Without disputing the director's freedom to make his own adaptation, we should note that this scene fits in with the general current of "repentance" sweeping Europe. Did not Willy Brandt kneel in front of the Warsaw Ghetto memorial? This is what Rosi himself argued, claiming to be in agreement with Primo Levi, who advocated remembering without hatred.

4. Teaching suggestions

You should raise the crucial question of the adaptation (faithful or a betrayal) whilst emphasising the fact that faithfulness is not a virtue in itself. Some brilliant adaptations of classic texts are very free, such as Orson Welles' *The Trial*. The important thing is to find equivalents which give the impression intended by the novelist. But adding to such a text scenes such as that with the German prisoner destroys the credibility and impact of a film which could have been highly regarded. It is not with crowds of famished-looking extras, black-and-white flashbacks, imaginary sentiments and grandiloquent speeches that a film-maker can convey this limbo so delicately depicted by the writer – that indefinable moment between despair and desire for life. Cinematic aestheticism might well amount to tactlessness in this case.

Werner Herzog, *Unbesiegbar (Invincible)*

Germany/United States/Britain/Ireland (2001), fiction, 133 min., colour; language: English

Historical theme: Rise of Nazism

Moral theme: two attitudes open to immigrants in a host country: assimilation or self-assertion

Aesthetic themes: political strength of myth and aesthetic use of myth in the cinema

The director

Born in Bavaria in 1942, Werner Herzog studied history and literature and decided to work night shifts as a welder to finance his first short film, which he made at the age of 19. To retain his independence, the film-maker endeavoured to be his own producer. In 1968 he made his first full-length film, *Signs of Life (Lebenszeichen)*, which won a special prize at the Berlin Film Festival. In 1973 *Aguirre, Wrath of God (Aguirre, der Zorn Gottes)* brought him international recognition. The director became one of the leading lights of German cinema together with Volker Schlöndorff, Reinhard Hauff and Rainer Werner Fassbinder. Despite his differences with the actor Klaus Kinski, he used him again in *Woyzeck* – presented in 1979 at the Cannes Film Festival, where in 1975 he had been awarded the Grand Prize of the Jury for *The Enigma of Kaspar Hauser (Jeder für sich und Gott gegen alle)* – and yet again in *Nosferatu the Vampyre (Nosferatu, Phantom der Nacht)*, a film which established Herzog as Murnau's heir. After having filmed in Africa on a number of occasions in the late 1960s *(Fata Morgana)*, he continued to make films abroad, such as *Fitzcarraldo* in 1982 (shot in Peru), *Where the Green Ants Dream* in 1984 (shot in Australia), and *Slave Coast* in 1988 (shot in Colombia and Ghana). In the 1990s he made a number of documentaries, including *My Best Fiend*, a portrait of his fetish actor Klaus Kinski, with whom he has always had a love-hate relationship on set. In 2001 *Invincible* was presented at the Venice Film Festival.

The film

1. Cast

Tim Roth: Hanussen

Jouko Ahola: Zishe Breitbart

Anna Gourari: Marta Farra

Max Raabe: Master of Ceremonies

Jacob Wein: Benjamin

2. Background

The film's hero, Zishe Breitbart, is a simple man, the tremendously strong son of a Jewish blacksmith. He is fair-haired and belongs to a very devout and close-knit Polish family. When an agent from Berlin offers him a chance to perform in Berlin one day he accepts – without any knowledge of show business. The idiosyncratic Hanussen, a cabaret manager and successful hypnotist who hopes to become the power behind the throne for the future Hitler government, hires him to personify the strength of the rising Germany under the name of Siegfried. Noting the rise of anti-Semitism, Zishe reveals his identity in public one evening and presents himself as the Jewish people's new Samson, thus giving fresh hope to the entire Berlin community.

3. Analysis

Werner Herzog is acutely aware of the cinematic power of myths ancient and modern, which he has portrayed unceasingly from Aguirre to Nosferatu by way of Kaspar Hauser and Fitzcarraldo. In *Invincible*, the second part of the portrait of Nazi Germany after Hanussen, he succeeds brilliantly in analysing the political use that Nazism made of myth. From Siegfried to Samson, the Colossus of Rhodes to Goliath, the great mythical figures of physical strength are summoned up by Herzog, who is concerned to contrast spiritual strength – in Hanussen and Zishe's young brother – with bodily strength. Moreover, as the simple young man (the primitive Kaspar Hauser in another guise) becomes more politically aware, he discovers that he has the gift of clairvoyance, likening him to the Greek Cassandra and the biblical prophets. A whole mythological universe thus informs this film, which reflects the dominant characteristics of Herzog's world and intends to show, with the plastic sense of the extravagant peculiar to the film-maker, how the Nazis used the German cultural heritage to further Hitler's seizure of power. But his main interest is perhaps in contrasting two basic attitudes of the Jewish people in the characters of Hanussen and Zishe: assimilation and self-assertion. Hanussen points out that a Jew only has a choice between two options: being run over like a dog, or adapting and merging into society. This is what we might call, in allusion to Woody Allen's film, the Zelig syndrome (from Zelig, the human chameleon). If he himself has chosen to take the second option to extremes by anticipating and foretelling the reign of fascism, it is because he is consumed by a visceral fear, unlike Zishe, whose strength protects him but who, like his young brother, embodies above all the calm assurance of the just.

4. Teaching suggestions

Students should be made aware of the omnipresent mythology in this film: classical mythology (Samson, Goliath, Cassandra, the prophets), the mythology dealt with in the director's work (Kaspar Hauser) and the Nazis' use of the German cultural heritage (Siegfried) to further Hitler's propaganda.

Costa-Gavras, *Amen*

France (2002), fiction, 133 min., colour; language: English; script written with Jean-Claude Grumberg

Historical themes: relationship between the papacy and the belligerent nations, the Pope's passivity

Moral theme: can one remain indifferent and passive at a time of war?

Aesthetic theme: historical reconstruction

The director

Born in Greece in 1933, Costa-Gavras moved to Paris in 1951. After studying literature at the Sorbonne he entered the French film school IDHEC. In the late 1950s he was an assistant to Henri Verneuil, René Clément, Jacques Demy and Jean Becker. In 1965 his first film *The Sleeping Car Murders* was a great success. There followed *Shock Troops* (1967) and *Z* (1969), the latter winning two Oscars and two awards at Cannes. This film was the first of a political trilogy which also includes *The Confession* (1971) and *State of Siege* (1973). Having thus specialised in political investigation, he won the Palme d'Or at the Cannes Festival and an Oscar for the best screenplay adaptation with *Missing* in 1981, before dealing with the theme of human rights violation in *Hanna K* (1983). Screenplays written in collaboration with Jorge Semprun and Franco Solinas, together with Yves Montand's name in the cast, guaranteed the success of Costa-Gavras's films. After trying his hand at a more intimate register in *Clair de Femme* (1979) and *Family Business* (1985) he abandoned film directing in order to attend to the Cinémathèque Française, of which he had been appointed president. *Betrayed* (1987) and *Music Box* (1989) marked his return to American cinema. *The Little Apocalypse* (1992) and *Mad City* (1996) went unremarked in the 1990s. In 2001 he made *Amen*, a historical drama which harks back to the commitment of his early films.

The film

1. Cast

Ulrich Tukur: Kurt Gerstein

Mathieu Kassovitz: Riccardo Fontana

Ulrich Mühe: the doctor

Michel Duchaussoy: the cardinal

Ion Caramitru: Count Fontana

Marcel Iures: the Pope

2. Background

A young mentally handicapped girl who has died without a plausible explanation kindles the suspicions of a German family, the Gersteins. A summary investigation reveals that she was in fact "euthanised" together with a number of other handicapped people, and the Church, scandalised, takes action in the person of the Cardinal of Westphalia, von Galen. A strong reprimand to the German authorities is enough to stop the process. The film is based on Rolf Hochhuth's German play from the 1960s, *The Deputy*, which tells the true story of Kurt Gerstein, an SS officer and hygiene specialist who supplied Zyklon B to the German army believing it to be intended for disinfection of premises. After realising the use that the Nazis wanted to make of it and having watched the gassing of prisoners, he tried to alert world opinion but without success.

It is a little-known fact from 1938 – the "euthanasia" of the disabled and mentally handicapped – that opens Costa-Gavras's most recent film, *Amen*. Costa-Gavras then comes to the extermination of the Jews, resolutely taking sides in the classic controversy concerning the culpability of Pius XII. He analyses his anguished nature, divided between vigilant and uncompromising anti-communism and the fear of Nazism; he shows him held back by his affection for Germany, where he had spent twelve years, and by his concern for a balance of power and for the Vatican's traditional neutrality. These are the preoccupations which prevented him from using his full moral weight to influence German policy. It must be acknowledged that he did not attempt to do so either when Poland was being laid waste and the Polish clergy were being ill-treated, or when he was given precise intelligence in 1942 about the mass elimination of the Jews, or during the arrest of Jews in Holland exposed by an apostolic letter, or when faced with the irrefutable eyewitness accounts of the Catholic Jan Karski, who was smuggled into the Warsaw Ghetto. No pressure, whether from inside or out, could overcome his impassibility. Confined behind the walls of his palace, the "good pastor", perfectly well acquainted with the existence of the gas chambers, felt obliged to protect only the treasures of Church art. Finally, in 1944, when the Hungarian Jews were the last to be taken to an extermination of which the whole world was aware, Pius XII did not seize this last chance to prevent large-scale slaughter. Although he knew all the details of Zyklon B and the gas chambers from an escaped Auschwitz prisoner, he contented himself with converting Jews in large numbers and sending a few safe-conducts, thus managing to save 5 000 Jews compared with the 400 000 who were gassed. This was the occasion on which he became the most closely involved.

3. Analysis

Costa-Gavras has made an impeccably rigorous and effective film. His regard for chronology and his precise information make it an excellent piece of historical fiction, simplified but generally accurate. We are familiar with this film-maker's talent for creating tense atmospheres and desperate situations, with no concessions

101

to pathos. By showing us the calvary of these two emblematic characters, the SS officer and the deputy, he indicates that the number of men of good will was tiny, their efforts were in vain and the world, including the United States, was aware of the extermination of the Jews. He also shows the unwieldiness of diplomatic rules, which prohibit any intervention even when millions of human lives are involved. As in the case of the disabled and mentally handicapped, however, it would probably have needed so little! A few rather more forceful and specific words from the Pope in his Christmas homily (in which the word "Jew" never occurred), some strong reprimands and a threat of excommunication addressed to Hitler's government. Admittedly, from 1943 onwards the Vatican saved a few Roman Jewish families of immediate concern to it by opening the convents, but it could have done so much more! Was it so difficult? What risk would the papal clergy really have run? These are the questions that the film asks.

4. Teaching suggestions

You should show how the portrayal of the Vatican as extremely well ordered, forming a contrast to the terrible news from the camps, helps Costa-Gavras to recount this German officer's desperate struggle against bureaucratic apathy and ecclesiastical diplomacy. Neither the Protestant authorities nor the Pope, informed by Gerstein, think it advisable to act. When Gerstein meets a young priest who is close to the Pope, this priest does his utmost to warn Pius XII, who does not react. Mathieu Kassovitz in the role of the increasingly disheartened priest is as convincing as Ulrich Tukur in the role of Gerstein. As for Michel Duchaussoy, he is excellent as an authoritarian Papal Nuncio and shrewd diplomat. Through their generosity and rigour, films such as this promote public awareness of the Shoah.

4. Anti-realism

Emmanuel Finkiel, *Voyages*

France (1999), 111 min., colour; language: French

Historical theme: aftermath of the Shoah

Moral theme: how to live after the Shoah

Aesthetic themes: triadic structure, memory and flashback, the present marked by the past, ellipsis, rejection of reconstruction

The director

Coming from a Jewish family that had experienced the camps, Emmanuel Finkiel was brought up with the memory of the Shoah and attempted unsuccessfully to enrol at the French film school IDHEC with a project concerning the deportation. Having trained as assistant director alongside film-makers such as Krzysztof Kieslowski, Christian de Chalonge, Bertrand Tavernier and Jean-Luc Godard, Emmanuel Finkiel had a noteworthy success with *Madame Jacques on the Croisette*, his first short film, in 1995. There followed *Voyages* in 1999 and *Casting* in 2000. These three films portray elderly Jews from a Yiddish culture today. They are consequently not documentaries about the Shoah but films about the present. The director said to journalists: "When I visited Auschwitz for the first time, what really struck me was that I could physically touch a stone. Touching this stone brought with it a sort of reality, which came from all the books about the camps that I had been able to read and look at." It is this continuation of the past in the present that interests the film-maker. The only reality for him is that of subjectivity. It is this which Finkiel endeavours to translate on screen by espousing the characters' point of view. In *Madame Jacques on the Croisette*, for example, the time in which the film is set is the time of those men and women who regularly come together in Cannes to talk of this and that, the one thing they have in common being their personal experience of the Shoah: a time both amplified and outside time for these people imprisoned in the bubble of their past.

The film

1. Cast

Shulamit Adar: Rivka

Esther Gorintin: Vera

Natan Cogan: Graneck

Mosko Alkalai: Shimon

Maurice Chevit: Mendelbaum

Michael Shillo: Monsieur Katz

2. Background

Voyages is a film devoted to those incredible old people who still throng the cafés of Tel Aviv: survivors of the camps, castaways of the diaspora, orphans of history. The director focuses on three women hunting for memories in three different stories set, respectively, on the way to Auschwitz, in Paris and in Tel Aviv. Each woman is trying to piece together the jigsaw of a memory full of holes. Each is linked to the two others. Rivka, who is 65, is a Frenchwoman who has moved to Israel and has now joined a tour group from Warsaw to Auschwitz; Régine, who is the same age and lives alone in Paris, receives into her home an elderly Lithuanian gentleman who claims to be her father; Vera, an 85-year-old Russian, has just emigrated to Israel to escape solitude by seeing her cousin again but feels lost in the streets of Tel Aviv.

3. Analysis

This triadic structure constitutes the strength of the film. It recreates that mosaic of time that Balzac tried to achieve by returning to the same characters. Each story seems both unique and part of a whole. Emmanuel Finkiel develops the submerged and barely discernible links between the three plots in both form and content. The narrative, which is linear, is meant to be nonchalant and matched to the pace of each character. On the frontier between documentary and fiction, using a number of non-professional actors, the film carefully avoids the temptations of overinsistent narration in favour of slices of life which unfold without any excessively conspicuous contrivances. Documentary is the director's influence and point of reference. He provides his stories with a framework and foundation all his own. The film-maker thus creates three characters strikingly true to life, who escape the script to lead a life of their own. The point of view is always restricted, so that the viewer cannot know or see more than the characters. Each of these characters is a prisoner of her own field of vision – for example, seeing of Poland only the stretch of landscape visible through the frost on the windows of the coach that is taking them to Auschwitz. To the film-maker's eye, reality consists of shots and sequences. Similarly, the inner world of each character is marked by what that character has experienced, which will determine the present, as in the case of the woman who was expecting so much of her life in Israel and finds herself as much a stranger there as anywhere else or the man who clings to the idea that he has found his daughter again until he receives clear proof to the contrary.

The path of the film is clearly emblematic: the route from Poland to France to Israel was taken by two generations in the middle of the 20th century. The theme of the return to one's roots here gives it a very special emotional value. The structure was thus determined by the subject itself. From one story to the next, the director demonstrates great virtuosity in changing viewpoints and his treatment of the characters. But his technique is harnessed to a very personal vision. These stories are not made-up fictions; they are fuelled by childhood memories, actual impressions and stories heard. For the director, the quest for identity is a family priority and a metaphysical worry, as if the fate of the Jewish people, suffered by his own family, were the tragedy of the human condition itself, doomed to finitude. In that case, the pursuit of happiness would be the most futile of illusions – or the impossible dream of a return to happy childhood.

At any rate, Emmanuel Finkiel has succeeded in finding his cinematic identity. Appealing to feelings and emotions, he is very sensitively carving out his own path in a cinema devoted to the models propagated by American cinema. The Shoah has become an obsession for him, a primal experience which has left an indelible mark on individual beings: melancholia.

4. Teaching suggestions

Part of the film's interest is to make us realise that it is possible to talk about the Shoah without showing it: no archival material, no historical reconstruction. The film's sensitive analysis is confined to the Shoah's present repercussions on individual lives. You might work on the restricted point of view, which makes each individual the prisoner of an inward focus while the director himself has an overall view of what connects these human beings. And you should show how the mental world of each of the characters is marked by the horrors that they have experienced, which are always off screen and hardly mentioned. This is a triumph of ellipsis over representation.

Yolande Zauberman, *La guerre à Paris (The War in Paris)*

France (2001), fiction, 90 min., colour; language: French

Historical theme: Paris under the Occupation

Moral theme: the choices to be made in a critical period

Aesthetic theme: anti-realism

The director

Yolande Zauberman began her career as a documentary-maker with acclaimed films such as *Classified People* (1988) and *Caste criminelle* (1990). She turned to fiction with *Ivan and Abraham* (1993) and *Clubbed to Death* (1996), films showing a strong documentary influence. For several years, in fact, she has been shooting "lyrical" documentaries which harmoniously blend reality with feeling. The common theme of her films is the crossing of a frontier between two worlds. Her narratives, set in distant countries or in Paris, deal with human beings rejected by society – outcasts. The yellow star, although not making an appearance, is the emblem of this here.

The film

1. Cast

Élodie Bouchez: Ana Maria

Jérémie Renier: Jules

Grégoire Colin: Commissaire Romain

Julien Le Gallou: Thomas

Jean-Pierre Léaud: man in high places

Hélène Lapiower: the mother

2. Background

The War in Paris is set in occupied France and has three young people as its protagonists. Jules and Thomas, 19 and 15 respectively, are Jewish. Their parents are in danger, but while Jules does not become involved in opposition to the Germans, Thomas dreams of fighting in the Resistance by the side of the young Spanish woman, Ana Maria, with whom he is in love. When Jules is only just saved from deportation by a French policeman who forces him to inform in order, ostensibly, to save his family he sinks into despair. How is he to escape the guilt that is consuming him?

3. Analysis

In the press, the director has stressed the fact that she particularly wanted to avoid historical reconstruction. It was not her aim to make a film about the persecutions that the Jews had suffered during the war. She wanted "to show the feelings physically experienced in the depths of their being by people caught up in extreme situations". Moreover, with Jules she has portrayed a young man who is different from the rest of his family (fair-haired and uncommitted) and who wishes to accept his own marginal status. The result? An intimate and impressionistic film where the presence of Paris is indicated by the outline of the dome of the Invalides in a car mirror, where the Jews have not yet bought their yellow stars and where the French are more active than the Germans in the role of persecutors. Freed thus from the tyranny of the set and doing away with any props that indicate discrimination too strongly, she allows us to get very close to these adolescents destroyed by the war, and this is an appreciable achievement.

4. Teaching suggestions

You should have the class look for all the signs of the political situation in occupied Paris during this period – signs which the director has intentionally reduced to a minimum. But it may be asked whether, although she succeeds in making tangible "the brutality of the unspoken" and the impossibility of communicating, she is not guilty of going to the opposite extreme by reducing dialogue to a murmur and action to an outline. Of course, ellipsis is here a moral and aesthetic choice and a result of the moral code adopted, but the narrative pattern seems to lead to unnecessary affectation. And for such a subject it would be immoral if the form were to cause the content to be forgotten.

Frederick Wiseman, *La dernière lettre (The Last Letter)*

France/United States (2002), docudrama, 61 min., black-and-white; language: French

Historical theme: massacre of a Jewish community in Russia

Moral themes: persecution and motherly love

Aesthetic themes: anti-realism, rejection of reconstruction, ellipsis

The director

Frederick Wiseman is one of the greatest documentary film-makers of our time. Born in Boston in 1930, he started by teaching law at Boston University but, preferring work in the field to work in the library, he visited prisons and followed trials with his students. His first film, *Titicut Follies* (1967), a documentary about the life of the criminally insane in a Massachusetts psychiatric hospital, caused a real shock by exposing the ancient premises, the lack of hygiene and care, and the violence. *Law and Order* (1969), *Basic Training* (1971), *Juvenile Court* (1973) and *Manoeuvre* (1979) continued to expose the state's "legitimate" violence. Among his more recent works we may mention *Near Death* (1989), *High School II* (1994), *La Comédie Française* (1996) and *Domestic Violence* (2001).

The film

1. Cast

Catherine Samie: the mother

2. Background

On 22 June 1941 Hitler broke the non-aggression pact with the USSR and launched an offensive on Soviet territory. Before long Ukraine and the Crimea were invaded, and the German army was at the gates of Leningrad, while the Jewish population in all these areas was exterminated. The town of Berdichev had 30 000 Jews among its 60 000 inhabitants. A third of them managed to escape before the Nazis entered the town on 7 July. The rest were all outlawed and confined to a ghetto before being savagely murdered from 4 to 14 September. In *Life and Fate*, written between 1954 and 1961, Vassily Grossman tells the story of a Stalingrad family from the Russian Revolution up to the Battle of Stalingrad, thus bringing back to life the history of a century which witnessed a paroxysm of human violence and in particular an eruption of anti-Semitic hatred. Confiscated by the KGB, the novel disappeared, but the text, smuggled out to the West as if by a miracle, was brought out in Switzerland in 1980 by the L'Age d'Homme publishing house before being reissued in France, Germany, Britain and the United States. Anti-Semitism is the main subject of the novel, whose most moving pages are those in which a Jewish doctor in Berdichev writes her son a last letter before being executed by the Nazis like all her co-religionists (Chapter 17).

3. Analysis

This text is partly autobiographical, since Vassily Grossman's mother died in Berdichev with the other inhabitants of the town. It was staged by Frederick Wiseman at the Comédie Française (the subject of another of his films). Persuaded of the topicality of this reflection on barbarity in our era – an era bestial beyond measure – he consequently wanted to bring it to the screen, and he gave the role of Anna Semionovna to Catherine Samie, one of the most remarkable actresses of the Comédie Française. She recites this letter, which the mother wrote inside the ghetto so that her son might know how she died and how she spent her last moments. The staging is therefore extremely simple: a fragile figure wearing a black dress on which the star is emblazoned; an emaciated and sorrowful face; hands held out or clenched tight; black and white; and the lighting, which lays bare the emotions and turns this figure into a shadow, both whole and symbolically fragmented, a silent tribute to all the shadows which haunt our modern age. This extremely stark film is a far cry from the cold statistics of the accountants or epic historical reconstructions. The words, superbly presented, carry a weight that no visual image could ever possess. They speak not of extermination but of the dehumanisation of the victims, treated like cattle, and of the profiteers who are even viler than the executioners inasmuch as they deprive the victims, on the threshold of death, of all human dignity and trust in humanity. These words conjure up the scanty comfort of seeming to find shelter from assailants in the bogus safety of the ghetto. They describe in detail the stubborn continuation of daily activities through habit or through an instinct to live, despite the increasingly imminent danger. They convey the indestructible strength of motherly love which enables this Mother Courage to find supreme consolation, in the midst of solitude, in the thought that her absent son is going to escape the slaughter. The barbarity is perceptible here only in the wild-eyed expression of this woman who is attempting to describe and understand it. It is off screen. And it constitutes the strength of the film, which requires its viewers and listeners to use their imagination to understand the weight of the words.

4. Teaching suggestions

You should show that among the film-makers who opt for meticulous reconstruction of events in polished images (such as Spielberg) and directors who opt for a more allusive and symbolic cinema (such as Roberto Benigni), Frederick Wiseman has found an obvious and dazzling solution: he shows nothing – nothing but an old woman, sensitive and intelligent, who makes desperate efforts to find the right words. The domestic and institutional violence which is this director's favourite theme is here pursued without its being shown. The whole skill of an exceptional director lies in the elegance of his choices: visual ellipsis, the reticence in the words of this woman who denies herself all pathos in order not to traumatise her absent son, and the director's respect for this dignified and resigned suffering. The scenes of slaughter remain subliminal, relegated to the locus of the collective unconscious. A figure suffused with light is sufficient to raise the dead and make heard the voices that were silenced. Catherine Samie, an inspired tragedian, becomes the universal mother whose boundless love cannot be killed. The Shoah becomes an intimate personal tragedy which touches us in the depths of our hearts, an everyday tragedy of persecuted innocence which makes us suddenly rebel. The film portrays a critical moment in the daily and eternal dialectic between master and slave, between love and hate, from which the victim emerges sanctified.

Marceline Loridan-Ivens, *La petite prairie aux bouleaux* *(The Little Birch-Tree Meadow)*

France (2003), docudrama, 90 min., colour; language: French

Historical theme: a survivor's return to Auschwitz sixty years later

Moral theme: impossibility of forgetting, and forgiveness

Aesthetic themes: anti-realism, film and repressed memory

The director

For the past twenty-five years Marceline Loridan has been the companion of the film-maker Joris Ivens, with whom she co-directed *A Tale of the Wind*. She is a documentary film-maker and has filmed all the wars of the past thirty years. As a child, she was arrested with her father in Bollène in 1943 and deported to Birkenau, where she lost some forty members of her family. In *The Birch-Tree Meadow* she returns to the camp aged 75, driven by the urgent need to pass on her experience and question her memory.

The film

1. Cast

Anouk Aimée: the survivor

August Diehl: the young German

Claire Maurier: Ginette

Marilu Marini: Suzanne

2. Background

The film's title sounds familiar. It may remind us of Wajda's *The Birch Wood*, an intimate film set in Poland and bearing no relation to the war. But the title of Loridan-Ivens' film is a literal translation of "Birkenau". After seeing a dinner of former prisoners in Paris, we are struck at first sight by the peaceful nature of the beautiful green and shady countryside. Marceline Loridan-Ivens enters the scene through Anouk Aimée, who plays the role of Myriam, the survivor, drawn to this place by the need to bear witness. Breaking in through the barely half-open gate of the women's camp so familiar to her, she opens up to us her personal experience and her memories.

3. Analysis

The main originality of the film is thus its form. Being a very sober piece of fiction, without reconstruction or flashbacks, whose protagonist is both real and imagined, it avoids the trap of a Hollywood *mise en scène*. But it is also meant to be a documentary on Birkenau today, the actual events that occurred there and the real emotions of a survivor confronted with her terrible past. This hybrid form will ruffle the feathers of documentary diehards and all those people who hold fiction about such a subject to be improper. But, to begin with, it is the only example of a film made by a survivor about what she herself experienced and is the first work made in Auschwitz itself. Furthermore, this form has invaluable qualities – above all that of discretion. In using Marceline's words to express herself and by speaking these words written over the years, Anouk frees Marceline from a morbid attitude to her suffering, which is conveyed but above all mediated. She thus distinctively expresses an individual, subjective, emotional and therefore unique point of view. Yet the viewer is moved more by the images than by the words. The director, conscious of the fact that cinema is now the universal language for handing down and assimilating history, has wanted to express herself in a language which is her own. Depriving the place of its sacred aura by filming nature, she asks the images to convey the guilt of the survivors (who owe their lives to the hazards of selection), the impossibility of forgetting and the triumph of life over death. She stages the symbolic encounter between Myriam and Oskar, a young German overwhelmed by the weight of inherited responsibility and eager to understand, as a confrontation between two worlds and between past and present.

4. Teaching suggestions

One of the most touching aspects of the film is its attempt to translate the workings of memory into words and images. On arrival, Myriam is immured in her grief and silence. Little by little, she opens up and becomes less inhibited through contact with the young man, realising that his own suffering is just as difficult to bear. Oskar helps Myriam to overcome her resistance. She even begins to recall for him recollections that had vanished from her memory. Doggedly repeating that she had dug the ground behind the kitchen, she gradually realises that she has invented a screen memory to repress the unendurable reality of the gas chamber, whose victims she had helped to bury. Scenes such as these are undoubtedly more striking than any number of painstaking reconstructions. This quest for memory and identity is thus all the more universal because it is more personal

PART FOUR

COMEDIES

Charles Chaplin, *The Great Dictator*

United States (1940), fiction, 124 min., black-and-white; language: English

Historical theme: the rise of Nazism

Moral theme: the temptation of absolute power and oppression of the weak

Aesthetic themes: parody, comedy, ellipsis

The director

Charles Spencer Chaplin was born in London in 1889 to parents who were music-hall entertainers and who separated when he was still quite young. He spent his childhood in great poverty. At the age of 10 he joined a troupe of child clog-dancers and subsequently became a member of Fred Karno's company until, in 1913, while touring the United States, he was spotted by the great Mack Sennett, who hired him for Hollywood. In the space of barely a year "Charlie Chaplin" became instantly famous. In 1918 Chaplin set up his own studio and the following year formed United Artists with his friends Douglas Fairbanks, Mary Pickford and D.W. Griffith. Various masterpieces followed (including *The Kid* and *The Gold Rush*), but talking pictures forced him to reconsider his career. Only in 1936 did he bow to circumstances with *Modern Times* but chose to express himself in song and in an incomprehensible gibberish. The film was such a success that the actor no longer had any choice. His next film was his first true talking picture: *The Great Dictator*. The script was finished on the eve of the declaration of war – on 1 September 1939 – and shooting was completed in March 1940 despite protests from the German ambassador and threats from pro-Nazi organisations and the House Un-American Activities Committee.

Although according to Truffaut, Chaplin's artistic expression found its perfect form in silent cinema, his work nevertheless loses none of its force when it moves to sound, and his voice becomes an additional asset, since it proves capable of creating intense emotion. He made three more films: *Monsieur Verdoux* in 1947, *Limelight* in 1952, and, finally, *A King in New York* in 1957. He spent his latter days in Switzerland, where he died in 1977 after having written two autobiographies.

The film

1. Cast

Charles Chaplin: Adenoid Hynkel/A Jewish barber

Paulette Goddard: Hannah

Jack Oakie: Napaloni (dictator of Bacteria)

Reginald Gardiner: Commander Schultz

2. Background

After the First World War, Hynkel, now dictator of Tomania, has undertaken to persecute the Jews. He clashes with Napaloni, an Italian dictator, who, like him, wants to invade Osterlich. Recovered after an accident, but amnesiac, a soldier who bears a striking likeness to Hynkel returns to his barber's shop in the ghetto unaware of all the changes that have taken place in his country. He there meets Hannah, with whom he falls in love. Persecution in the ghetto leads the barber to confront Hynkel's commandos without realising the risk that he is running. Chance, and above all the resemblance between the two men, mean that Hynkel is arrested by his own troops and the barber is mistaken for the dictator, which gives him an opportunity to deliver a marathon speech.

3. Analysis

The film portrays two unscrupulous megalomaniacs, prisoners of their own images and their thirst for power, trapped in a vicious circle: too much power makes them lose their heads and, having lost their heads, they demand even more power. This classic film, a critique of power divorced from reality, is both a thoroughly successful comedy and a hymn to tolerance. Neither grossly caricaturing the ghetto, nor exaggerating the humanist portrayal of better feelings, Chaplin handles satire in masterly fashion. But the film-maker's first talking picture still handles visual language above all. This is the last typical Charlie Chaplin film, relying on extremely visual gags and a pace which prolongs and intensifies the comic effects, thus increasing their impact. The tramp remains silent right until the end, while his double harangues the crowds as if to underline the director's farewell to silent cinema and his regretful conversion. From the sequence around the big gun to the wild escapade in the aeroplane, from the raid in the ghetto to the improvised shaving in time to a Brahms Hungarian dance, from the extremely poetic scene of Hynkel juggling with a globe to the ludicrous interview between the two dictators, slapstick and situation comedy reign supreme. But verbal comedy is everywhere in Hynkel's speeches, made hilarious as much by the bombast of his xenophobic vocabulary as by Chaplin's body language. The systematic paronymy of proper names adds further comic effect to the running theme of the confusion between Hynkel and the barber. Last but not least, the film is very carefully paced. Long shots, sometimes almost becoming a sequence, set out to establish continuity of action through dissolves. However, Chaplin is able to speed up his story to reflect the tide of history; the passage of time between the two world wars is indicated by jump cutting, which allows him to conjure up twenty years of history whilst not passing over any important events. Then the long shots return, ending with a final marathon monologue lasting eight minutes.

The Great Dictator is a universally relevant hymn to tolerance. As early as 1940, Chaplin, who was militant in his opinions, asserted the equality of blacks and whites and all men in general. The alienation of man by the machine (here the war machine) again puts in an appearance – following *Modern Times* four years earlier – as one of the director's great preoccupations. The final speech, that huge epilogue, is a veritable purple passage which takes the place, contrary to all expectations, of the final confrontation between the two men with moustaches. For eight minutes Chaplin no longer addresses the military audience but speaks direct to camera and therefore to the viewer. This speech is the brilliant idea which solves the problem of the transition from silent to sound cinema. Its intensity comes from its unflagging pace throughout, its generous message and the striking contrast with the speeches of the dictator Hynkel. Transfiguring the self-effacing hero and transcending time and space, it takes up the link between voice and image and makes it mankind's salvation. Yet this final speech has a significance which is even more subtle. Has the Jewish barber involuntarily become a dictator of the spoken word? The violence of the closing words make you wonder whether this liberating speech is not the first sign of a new dictatorship in which expression will be appropriated by a single man, a speaker intoxicated by his own eloquence. We can see how Chaplin's discovery of talking pictures is an opportunity for questioning the power of speech. It leads him to meditate on the limits to his own speech and the deviations which he himself is trying out: "I'm sorry but I don't want to be an emperor – that's not my business – I don't want to rule or conquer anyone. I should like to help everyone if possible, Jew, gentile, black man, white. We all want to help one another, human beings are like that. We all want to live by each other's happiness, not by each other's misery. We don't want to hate and despise one another. In this world there is room for everyone and the earth is rich and can provide for everyone. The way of life can be free and beautiful. But we have lost the way."

4. Teaching suggestions

Taking the famous scenes, it is easy to analyse the different forms of comedy and show their effectiveness as a way of presenting ideas in this process of argument. But you must also demonstrate how comedy is transcended by the humanist ideal that is first apparent in the barber's actions and subsequently in his final speech. Ideally, you should present *The Great Dictator* and Benigni's *Life Is Beautiful* in two consecutive showings in order to illustrate the formal similarity between these two films in their use of comedy (see entry on Benigni).

Ernst Lubitsch, *To Be or Not to Be*

United States (1942), 100 min., black-and-white; language: English

Historical theme: German occupation of Warsaw and annexation of Poland

Aesthetic themes: comedy as satire, parody and an effective means of exposing dictatorship; mixture of genres, mirror story

The director

Born in Berlin on 28 January 1892, Ernst Lubitsch is one of those European Jewish directors who were the true face of Hollywood. He initially worked in the theatre as an actor with Max Reinhardt before starting to make films. In 1922, after having directed a large number of films in Germany, including those with Pola Negri (*Gypsy Blood* and *Passion*), he was invited by Mary Pickford to the United States, where he made all his masterpieces. Particular mention may be made of *One Hour with You* and *Trouble in Paradise* (1932), *Ninotchka* (1939), *The Shop Around the Corner* (1940), *To Be or Not to Be* (1942), *Heaven Can Wait* (1942) and *Cluny Brown* (1947). Heart problems prevented him from having complete control over his last films, and he died in California on 30 November 1947 without completing *That Lady in Ermine*. What has been called the "Lubitsch touch" is the incredible lightness with which he handles vaudeville and comedy of manners whilst introducing serious political, and even philosophical, reflections. *To Be or Not to Be* is an excellent example of this balance.

The film

1. Cast

Jack Benny: Joseph Tura

Carole Lombard: Maria Tura

Robert Stack: Lieutenant Sobinski

2. Background

In Warsaw in August 1939, Joseph Tura's theatrical troupe is putting on a play called *Gestapo*. It is banned, however, and so the actors switch to *Hamlet*, with Joseph Tura as the Prince of Denmark. A young lieutenant has fallen in love with Joseph Tura's wife, who takes advantage of the "To be or not to be" monologue to receive him in her dressing room. All the characters become involved in a very dangerous affair of espionage, from which they emerge with flying colours.

3. Analysis

This film came out two years after Chaplin's *The Great Dictator*. Its setting is the city of Warsaw at that particularly tragic moment in history when the Nazis were invading Poland. The film begins with a scene which is both satirical and very funny: the presence of Hitler in a Warsaw street in the midst of dumbfounded passers-by. This is an introduction which plunges us into the heart of the matter – the lack of distinction between theatre and the reality to which it makes reference, and between the actors and their historical characters – since the play *Gestapo* is too much akin to political reality not to offend the occupation authorities, and the actor who plays Hitler is so true to life that anybody might be taken in. This is doubtless an allusion to the isolationists in the United States, who, prior to Pearl Harbor, condemned all anti-Nazi films (including *The Great Dictator*) as anti-American.

The film's stroke of genius is to have elaborately crossed classic vaudeville – the deceived husband, the young and impetuous lover and the fickle woman – with a spy story set in occupied Poland. Furthermore, the vaudeville protagonists are simultaneously actors on the stage and players in a real-life political intrigue. Suspense is at its height when the young lieutenant returns secretly from London to prevent a spy from handing over members of the Resistance. As a result, each member of the company plays a role for which he or she has been prepared through rehearsals for the banned play. The touchiness of the actor Joseph Tura almost makes him forget his jealousy, and his jealousy overshadows the actual danger of the visit to the Gestapo. Unfortunately this burlesque shocked the American press and public opinion, which accused Lubitsch of having mixed up his genres by combining drama with comical satire, having jeopardised the war effort by underestimating the danger of the Nazis, and having been tactless in choosing Warsaw as the setting for his film. He replied in the *New York Times* of 29 March 1942 that he had wanted to make a "tragic farce" or a "burlesque tragedy". And he added: "No actual torture chamber is photographed, no flogging is shown, no close-up of excited Nazis using their whip and rolling their eyes in lust. My Nazis are different; they passed that stage long ago. Brutality, flogging, and torturing have become their daily routine." And a Nazi officer is delighted to hear himself nicknamed "concentration camp" because he is their best purveyor.

4. Teaching suggestions

You should show with what ease Lubitsch plays with verbal comedy, superposing images with erotic connotations (lock/key, shepherd/sheep) on the cryptic metaphors of the spy film. You should point out that Shakespeare is a favoured source of intertextuality in this film, which turns Hamlet's soliloquy into an opportunity for adultery and makes it the lovers' secret code, mistaken for a political code. But Shylock's speech about the Jews also returns as a leitmotiv to characterise the fate of the Polish people being martyred by the Nazis. Last but not least, an officer laughs heartily as he says of the actor Tura, "What he did to Shakespeare we are doing to Poland." This film is a perfect example of a mirror story or theatre within theatre. Lubitsch thus succeeds in confusing us and making it impossible to distinguish between true and false Nazis, between true and false beards, and between the theatre company and the SS army. The Nazi *mise en scène* seems more of a parody than the play itself. And the key scenes from Hamlet are so closely connected with the plot that they end up by becoming part of it. This is great art.

Roberto Benigni, *La vita è bella (Life Is Beautiful)*

Italy (1997), fable, 117 min., colour; language: Italian

Historical themes: rise of Nazism, concentration camps, the "final solution"

Aesthetic themes: fable, rejection of realism, humour, understatement

The director

Born in Tuscany in 1952, Roberto Benigni begins his career in cabaret and then on television as a comic. A worthy heir of *commedia dell'arte*, he exploits his long-limbed body and his persona of a dazed, rubber-faced clown. His humour is rooted in social reality, which quickly puts him on the audience's side. Often naïve or dreamers, the characters that he plays are engaging on that account. Whether as victim (*The Monster*, which he directed in 1994, in which public opinion wrongly believes him guilty of some heinous murders) or as militant (*You Upset Me*, 1983, in which he exposes the workings of the capitalist system, or *Johnny Toothpick*, in which he plays the naïve double of a dangerous criminal, allowing him to make delightful mockery of the Mafia), he is effective and appreciated.

While this provocation and caustic humour initially upset and frightened the cinema world of the early 1980s, Benigni is now accepted as one of the greatest Italian directors on account of his undeniable subtlety and intelligence. The enormous public success of his comedies has led him to act for the greatest of film-makers such as Bertolucci, Costa-Gavras, Jarmush and Fellini. But it was in *Life Is Beautiful*, which received the Grand Prize of the Jury at the Cannes Film Festival, that his sensitivity found full expression, drawing inspiration from the unassuming reticence of his father, who was an inmate of the Bergen-Belsen camp from 1943 to 1945. In its rejection of special effects and its jerky pace, *Pinocchio* (2002) revives the comedy of *commedia dell'arte*, yet at the same time sublimating it by a depth worthy of this work so pregnant with meaning.

The film

1. Cast

Roberto Benigni: Guido Orefice

Nicoletta Braschi: Dora

Giorgio Cantarini: Giosué

Giustino Durano: Eliseo Orefice

Sergio Bini Bustric: Ferruccio Papini

Horst Buchholz: Dr Lessing

2. Background

In 1938 Guido comes to the city with his cousin Ferruccio looking for work. On the way, he meets Dora, a beautiful school teacher, who happens to fall into his arms. Henceforth he can think only of her. The young man and his relatives, who are Jewish, have to face anti-Semitism. To win the woman he loves, Guido bursts into Dora's wedding (on horseback) where she is being forced to marry a fascist dignitary and carries her off!

Five years later they have become the parents of little Giosué. Guido is a bookseller and, faced with increasingly violent persecution and exactions, he lies to his son in order not to disturb him and makes a joke of everything – up to the day when the whole family finds itself in a concentration camp. Guido persists in his determination to lie, in order to protect his son from the horror, presenting the camp as the setting for a huge game in which he must follow the rules laid down by the German guards, whose manners are admittedly sometimes a little unpolished. Through various sleights of hand the illusion is maintained, although the child is not entirely taken in. Guido weathers the worst ordeals, managing to make contact with his wife and hide his son. But the Allies are approaching. Guido is summarily executed, the Germans flee, the prisoners are left to their own devices, and Giosué, now alone, is saved by the arrival of the Americans. Having become an adult, he tell us this incredible tale.

3. Analysis

Like *The Great Dictator*, Roberto Benigni's *Life Is Beautiful* is an atypical film about the Shoah. But it raised a real outcry of indignation among international critics. Why?

If *Life Is Beautiful* caused such controversy upon its release, it was because people were afraid of seeing this impossible subject being treated lightly or even casually. Some people even felt that cinema was not fit to deal with it – especially in the comic register. The incomprehension manifested by many critics and cinemagoers appears to stem from various misunderstandings. What is at issue here is the status of cinema, the status of fiction and the status of comedy, which must be clarified. It is essential to point out that Benigni's film should be defined as a fable, a fairy tale, or, I would say, even a philosophical *conte* comparable to Voltaire's *Candide*, for example. Reality serves merely as a backdrop or pretext for a meditation on barbarism.

Benigni has learned the lesson of non-realism from Charlie Chaplin and included reminders of *The Great Dictator* in his film:

–   the systematic paronymy of proper names (in *The Great Dictator*, Adenoid Hynkel, Ben Napaloni, etc.). This paronymy becomes biblical, mythical and metaphysical for Benigni, who calls his main character Guido, the guide – the positive alter ego of the *Führer* – and gives him the surname Orefice, "goldsmith" (who turns everything to gold); his son is Giosué (Joshua), like the biblical hero who reaches the promised land instead of Abraham; his uncle is Eliseo (Elisha), like the prophet; his wife is Dora, a name which recalls the Greek word "gift" and gold (aurum);

–   the motif of the comic misidentification: the barber in *The Great Dictator* is mistaken for Hynkel; Guido is mistaken for the Minister of Education;

–   visual and verbal clowning in the most desperate situations;

–   non-realistic *mise en scène* of the camp.

Benigni realised that in a period sated with media news, realism was a non-starter for a cinema audience whose feelings had been blunted by a surfeit of horror. He therefore chose a different path: not the real or the plausible but rather anti-realism and artifice, together with symbolism, as learnt from Chaplin and Fellini. How empty and redundant a discussion of the accuracy of historical details or the film's comic approach then becomes – a film which the director presents from the outset as a fable, a fairy tale! Benigni has invented an allegory whose *mise en scène* features two main characters: the fool who, with his innate simplicity, reveals the cruelty and absurdity of the world, and the child, who is innocent enough to see things as they are. Between these two characters there is the presence of the noble lie, the game, that is, the imagination. The message conveyed by Benigni in his film is that man is a reed, the weakest in the universe. The whole world may take up arms to destroy him and yet he is superior to what is killing him in being able to think and deny. Only Pascal can truly express what we feel on seeing this film. What it portrays is a human being's specific ability to master the most terrible of situations through thought. The game devised by the father to enable his son to endure an unendurable life is the most sophisticated form of thought. For games, according to Roger Caillois, are accompanied by an awareness of an alternative reality or actual unreality in relation to everyday life. To play is to enter into an illusion. It is "make-believe". But once this illusion has been established, it becomes reality for the player. Altering his son's apprehension of reality, such is the intention of this admirable father who has understood his educational role in the most noble sense. Like a poet, he arranges the elements of this appalling world to make a new kind of order for his son which is not only acceptable but also jubilant. This is demonstrated by certain emblematic sequences: the sequence in which he translates the initial SS orders to the camp's new arrivals into the rules of the game, and above all the sequence in which the child begins to have his doubts, having heard that the Nazis gas prisoners, burn their corpses and turn them into buttons and soap, and Guido derides these acts as absurd, inhuman and unthinkable – which, in actual fact, they are.

4. Teaching suggestions

It is this victory of the human spirit, greater than whatever oppresses it, that is Roberto Benigni's message to men throughout the ages. You should point out the perfect consistency of the lie, which is what makes its staging successful. The film thus establishes an illusion which bears witness to the strength of the imagination in triumphing over adversity. Moreover, humour is a very sophisticated form of thought, which the Jews have carried to perfection. It consists in holding reality at a distance and laughing at it in order to lessen its traumatising force. Although Guido does not make jokes but is continually endeavouring to conceal the horror from his child by turning each event into a stage of the game, humour is nevertheless present in the constant distance established by the character not only between the waking dream and the reality but also between his true nature and the roles that he is playing. With unrivalled tenderness he is constantly splitting himself into two and acting a part, even at the times when he is most exhausted. This desperate game that he organises in order to protect his son from the terrible reality here appears as the highest form of fatherly devotion. These are the ethical and aesthetic questions raised by the film. But, above all, it is a great film, which has found an original aesthetic solution to the problem of representation and has thus shown that art is the only answer to every question and the best way of handling such a subject.

Chantal Akerman, *Demain on déménage (Tomorrow We Move)*

Belgium (2004), 110 min., colour; language: French

Historical theme: existential problems of third generation after the Shoah

Aesthetic themes: comedy, ellipsis, lightness of touch

The director

Chantal Akerman was born in Brussels on 6 June 1950. After having seen Jean-Luc Godard's *Pierrot le fou* she enrolled at INSAS, the Belgian film school. Her initial career was marked by experimentation after a stay in New York and her discovery of the American avant-garde. She has retained a liking for its use of sound and static shots in films virtually devoid of action, such as *Jeanne Dielman* (1975), a 200-minute film about the life of a Belgian housewife, a casual prostitute who discovers pleasure. In *The Meetings of Anna* (1978), she tracks a young woman film-maker (played by Aurore Clément) who is travelling in Europe. Although still a documentary-maker, Chantal Akerman has tried her hand at every genre. *Golden Eighties* (1986), following *The Eighties* (1983), is a wink at musical comedy. *American Stories: Food, Family and Philosophy* (1989) conjures up the American Jewish diaspora and its efforts to recapture the memory of the time before the camps. *The Captive* (2000) is a remarkable adaptation of Proust's novel of the same name.

The film

1. Cast

Sylvie Testud: Charlotte

Aurore Clément: Catherine

Jean-Pierre Marielle: Popernick

Natacha Régnier: pregnant woman

Lucas Belvaux: Monsieur Delacre

2. Background

After her husband's death, a mother returns to live with her daughter, who is single and writes erotic novels, in the new flat which they have bought, but they immediately decide to resell it. The round of prospective buyers will change their lives.

3. Analysis

A concert grand is lifted off the ground by two cables before the apprehensive gaze of the bystanders. A woman follows it up to the sixth floor, where she is moving in. She plays it straight away, while her daughter, notebook in hand, notes down everything that is said. The film plunges us into a removal and into the midst of some eccentric characters. Dust, chaos and commotion.

Two artists unconcerned about material things and inclined to seize the opportunity to make friends negotiate this shambles in blissful oblivion. The mother gives piano lessons, and the daughter is without a lover despite her occupation of erotic novelist. She is continually chasing ideas, but what she actually records in her precious pocket-book are words, scraps of sentences, and set expressions – the randomness of received ideas. A veritable sponge, she absorbs all the language of everyday life, especially advertising jargon and sales patter. This verbal hotchpotch takes on a new meaning in her mouth when she uses it appropriately.

In this hilarious comedy Chantal Akerman is following Ionesco in orchestrating a succession of visitors to the flat that is being sold no sooner than it has been bought, but she is actually talking about something that has always haunted her, namely the Shoah. Is the third generation really less scarred than the two previous ones? Poland is the backdrop to this Parisian comedy, present as much in the disinfectant smell of the two-room flat being visited as in the black smoke issuing from the oven and the smoke extractor. However, the visitors drink coffee and talk about music, couples break up and everybody seeks happiness, in spite of everything, in the welcoming atmosphere of this flat which its owners are trying in vain to get under control. This is a light comedy in appearance only; it is founded on tragedy, being a serious comedy about general discomfort and the oppressive legacy borne by the two women and their new friend Popernick, who is too depressed not to drive everybody who meets him to despair. The generations' incompatibility of temperament also arises from this heavy inheritance of grief. Luckily the lorry which removes the piano once again belongs to the Mazel company (*mazel* meaning "luck" in Hebrew!).

4. Teaching suggestions

You should get the class to note all the – barely discernible – allusions to a traumatising past actually experienced or just apprehended. And you should show how comedy can treat such a serious subject lightly by turning pessimism into humour and the weight of past experience into song. The obliviousness of these two women is doubtless the result of a life which has taught them that only really vital matters are worth worrying about. What is in the memories of children and grandchildren is no less painful than what is in the survivors' memories. We should remember the comment of another contemporary film-maker: "When I talk to you about Auschwitz, it is not from deep memory my words issue. They come from external memory, if I may put it that way, from intellectual memory, the memory connected with thinking processes. Deep memory preserves sensations, physical imprints. It is the memory of the senses."[43]

---

43. Charlotte Delbo, *Days and Memory,* translated by Rosette Lamont, Marlboro Press, 1990.

Sales agents for publications of the Council of Europe
Agents de vente des publications du Conseil de l'Europe